SUPERHUMAN
BEING

SUPERHUMAN BEING

BE BOLD
BE IMPERFECT
BE PRESENT
AND RECOVER

L. J. WINTER

Library of Congress Control Number: 2023901431

Paperback ISBN: 979-8-9870127-1-0
Hardcover ISBN: 979-8-9870127-0-3
eBook ISBN: 979-8-9870127-2-7

SEL 043000 SELF-HELP/Post Traumatic Stress Disorder
SEL 020000 SELF-HELP/Mood Disorders/Depression
PSY 036000 PSYCHOLOGY/Mental Health

Cover design and typesetting by Kaitlin Barwick
Edited by James Alf and Emily Chambers

ljw@superhumanbeing.net
http://superhumanbeing.net

TO MY WIFE,
WHO MAKES ME FEEL SAFE
AS I PURSUE MY PATHWAY TO WHOLENESS

CONTENTS

CONTENTS

FOREWORD

When I first met L. J., I was struck by the fact that he was a man on a mission—a mission to help others heal and continue to be present in their mental health recovery journey. He told me at our early meetings about how he wanted to write a book that helped to eliminate the negative stigma of mental health conditions, addictions, and trauma. He had this idea that we as humans are, at our core, imperfect. There is no such thing as being in perfect mental health. However, being open to the present moment is a way to heal and feel less alone. He mentioned being a SuperHuman Being and how his own healing was an important part of this new understanding of what it means to be human.

Being a mental health professional for more than two decades, L. J. has not only had the practical experience to shed light on how one might manage depression, anxiety, bipolar, addiction, trauma, and other mental health conditions but also shares his own recovery journey and his commitment to stay on a path of recovery.

The stigma that many face from having a mental health condition can feel isolating and make it difficult to seek the help and connections to others that we need in order to grow and transform. L. J. helps us know that we are not alone and that there is a way to be a SuperHuman Being—even though we feel imperfect.

As we discussed the ideas for his book when he first began his writing journey, he saw how much healing was available not only to his readers but to himself as well.

In 2022, according to Mental Health America, 19.86% of adults are experiencing a mental illness. **Equivalent to nearly 50 million Americans** and 4.91% are experiencing a *severe* mental illness.[1] That means one out of four people is suffering from some form of mental illness. In a nuclear family of four, that means it's probably someone in your own family or yourself. However, people are still not comfortable discussing this issue, which might be affecting their ability to live and thrive in their communities.

L. J. has written a book that addresses the SuperHuman qualities one already has inside of them to begin to heal and to remain on the road to recovery. He is a wonderful and honest guide for anyone looking for the peace that comes from starting and maintaining the journey of recovery. This book is the perfect remedy for anyone who is on the path to healing and is willing to be bold, imperfect, present, and recover.

AZUL TERRONEZ

TEDX SPEAKER AND *WALL STREET JOURNAL* & *USA TODAY* BESTSELLER

NOTE

1. "Adult Prevalence of Mental Illness (AMI) 2022," MHA, https://mhanational .org/issues/2022/mental-health-america-adult-data#two.

INTRODUCTION

This book came about due to my lifelong journey with a mental health condition and the impact of abuse. I am one of the millions that suffer from these experiences in the United States. This book was inspired by my own lived experience with severe depression, anxiety, physical and emotional abuse, addiction, and trauma. It also comes about from my mom's lifelong struggle with bipolar disorder. My father has encouraged me over the last decade to write down our family's story.

Like the superheroes from our youth, the title *SuperHuman Being* is most fitting for this work. Most heroes share some common values, like courage, strength, and intelligence. But they will also have several dominant qualities which help to define their unique personalities. I believe when you or someone you care about elects to recovery they are a SuperHuman Being.

I want to join my voice with those who suffer from a mental health condition, abuse, and/or addiction, and those who struggle to understand what living with a mental health condition, abuse, and/or addiction is like. Recovery is a lifetime journey, not a sole event; there is no "one and done" for us.

After more than fifty years of suffering, I now realize there is no cure. Instead, the goal of psychiatric treatment should be to treat and support a mental health condition, addiction, and trauma. The relationships, techniques, medications, and skills that work best for one person may not be the same antidote that works for another person. The good news is that a pathway exists for each one of us to lead a productive life. Writing this book was transformational for me. It is full of hope, healing, and health as demonstrated by my lived experience. I want the book to be difficult for you to put down once you begin reading it.

My birth was the uncorking of my mother's own struggle with bipolar disorder and my dad's unresolved childhood physical and emotional abuse. Recovery makes all things possible for us. On the other hand, recovery is frustrating, exhausting, and a host of other verbs you may use to describe your own experiences.

The book is broken down into four parts each representing the qualities of a truly remarkable person. The first one is to BE BOLD, meaning it takes courage to step forward and say to yourself I want to feel better. The second part is to BE IMPERFECT, admitting to ourselves that because of our humanity we never will be perfect on this side of heaven. To BE PRESENT means being aware of your surroundings and what you are feeling rather than escaping into social media, alcohol, drugs, trying to change others, and other unhealthy behaviors. The final part of this book is to RECOVER, to regain health, balance, and control in your life.

Sometimes before watching a movie, I watch the trailer, which shows highlights of the film. Once I have an idea of what the film encompasses, I make a decision whether spending two hours watching it is worth my time.

The first chapter is a synopsis of what to expect in the subsequent work. I am giving you a few snippets to tickle your curiosity to read on. My birth is the tip-off of my development like the beginning of a basketball game.

PART ONE

BE BOLD

CHAPTER 1

BEGINNING TIP-OFF

Recovery Begins

Have you ever thought to yourself, "How did I get to this point in my life?" Each person has a distinct gene pool and background. I invite you to join me in reviewing my childhood and adult circumstances. You'll read about challenges during my lifetime that caused emotional scarring, and I want you to benefit from the ways I found healing.

I worked as a social worker for thirty years before retiring in November 2018. My doctors had advised me to give up work due to several medical conditions. So, at the age of fifty-five, I resigned as Director of Human Services for a Wisconsin county. When I retired, people asked me, "What are you going to do now?" My response was simple: "Get healthy."

The line, "You have come a long way baby (Larry)" is applicable to my pathway of healing. If we were in a room together you might query what my life was like. My answer is when I began healing in my thirties, it was like a tango dance. I tried several treatments, consumed various medications, and attended support groups; but I could not find the right partner. Finally, in April 2015, I found a therapist with expertise in Eye Movement Desensitization and Reprocessing therapy (EMDR) to help me heal from childhood physical and emotional abuse and trauma. You will learn more about this in chapter eight. I found hope, healing, and health with the support of a therapist. The emotional wounds have healed, but I continue to carry the memories in my mind of the events that occurred in my childhood. With that said, the years of emotional anguish are now over.

Warning: If you become overwhelmed by the content of this work, I recommend seeking support from those who love you, a support group, or a professional.

My parents are mentioned throughout this book. I no longer hold deep-seated anger, bitterness, or malice toward them. I have forgiven them and extended mercy to them. How did I accomplish this? By working through a twelve-step program, which you will find in the appendix of this book.

Mom passed away in June of 2021. Prior to her death, I often visited her at an assisted living facility. We had a good relationship for several years prior to her passing away. Some of the things we discussed will be woven into the story you are about to read. Dad is a healthy eighty-four-year-old man and lives next door to my wife and me. I assist him with his finances, medical issues, and other needs he may have. There will be references to the despicable things he did to me. These memories are mine, and I take full responsibility for my recall of what actually happened. Today he is loving toward me, is very gentle with me, is pleasant and safe to be with, and adores children.

In this book, I will discuss the connection between mental and physical health. Prior to that time, I was clueless about any connection between these two functions of my body. After years of suffering from a mental health condition, my physical body began to fail. My physical health steadily declined from 2015 thru 2020. It began with severe constipation, then, I was diagnosed with severe osteoporosis, and a pituitary tumor in my brain. Eventually, my physical decline caused me to leave the social work profession I loved. Now I dedicate my time to addressing the root causes of my mental and physical conditions, being a husband and a father, and supporting recoverers.

According to social security, I am disabled. I still find this label hard to accept due to my pride. On the other hand, I feel blessed to be alive and have the financial means to take care of my family and our mental, emotional, and physical health. I am thankful to society for monetarily supporting people like me with disabilities.

Due to Mom's mental health condition, she no longer was able to work as a nursing assistant. She left the profession in her mid-twenties. Soon after I was born, she was diagnosed with bipolar disorder. Her illness began impacting my growth and development as a child and my dad's role in the family. After she left employment, she qualified for Social Security Disability, which helped our family to financially survive.

You may be shocked by some of the stories you will read. These stories are true and accurate based on my recollections of what occurred. Nonetheless, they are important to tell so that you can understand the interconnection between the mental, emotional, and physical health in our family and the impact on my life.

Do you have a family member or friend who suffers from a mental health condition, abuse, or addiction? If so, I hope you discover by reading this work that you are not alone. Sharing our family's story may help you normalize your experience and reduce any stigma you may be undergoing.

Despite all the trauma, there were moments when my parents treated me well. For years I fixated on the doom and gloom in our family. Finally, at age fifty-one, I committed to healing. As I heal, the dark and tragic events lose their power and grip on my mind.

I played a lot of basketball as a child, youth, and young adult. This was a coping strategy I used to channel my feelings in a prosocial manner. As you turn the pages of this book, you will find both positive and negative experiences from my participation in sports. As the years drifted by, basketball became an addiction for me. It led to a number of unhealthy behaviors. If you have an unhealthy relationship with exercise, you may be able to relate to this.

I will introduce you to a few men that mentored me. Whenever I experienced a dark mood, I benefited from their sage advice. I could count on them to help me through an emotional event. If this book were written thirty-five years ago, I would have viewed them as a dad rather than mentors. There were other men who did not treat me well. I endured emotional consequences because of their harsh behavior toward me.

I was fifty-one years old before I realized I suffered from childhood trauma. A psychologist I connected with brought this to my attention. During the later years of my career as a social worker, I went to several workshops on the topic of trauma. I did not apply what I was learning to my condition because I was in denial. Once I identified my own trauma, I said to myself, "Okay now, what do I do about it?"

The trials and tribulations of depression and anxiety have raised my compassion toward others and how I view myself. I sense when people are in pain and offer to listen to their stories. For this reason, I began a "Peer Recovery Support Group."[1] I am at a level of healing whereby I can offer love and support to those who are going through the same struggles I labor over. Doing so motivates me to keep taking care of myself so that I remain in remission and strive to become a whole person.

Recovery is a process of change through which I am improving my health and wellness, figuring out the path I want to take, and becoming the best version of myself. I seek advice from my care team rather than solely relying on myself. I have carefully chosen people willing to commit to helping me heal.[2]

After years of silence and shaming myself, now I focus on my strengths. I am kind, compassionate, have a love for learning, take responsibility for my actions, have the ability to connect with people or groups, and enjoy writing.

I do not want to be a burden to people. I need people to provide me with the tools necessary to empower me to improve my health. I seek out those who would suggest different means to manage my mental and physical conditions, allowing me to take what I want and leave the rest.

Despite retiring earlier than I wanted to, I am creating new meaning and purpose in my life. I am deepening my relationship with God, serving my family, facilitating a Peer Support Group for those like me in recovery, writing, and becoming an author. Arriving at this place has not been easy, but family and friends' encouragement has been very helpful to me.

As you begin to read my work you will find one constant throughout the book. I held onto hope and am willing to exert myself to heal. For most of my life, hope and resiliency were chief components of my survival. See if you can pick out the moments when hope and resiliency are evident in the upcoming stories.

Optimism is a guiding principle of recovery. Do you remember the attitude of the little train? "I think I can, I think I can." I've revised it to say, "I know I can, I know I can." I take it one day at a time. This attitude brings me confidence that regardless of what the future holds for me, "I know I can, I know I can."

Gaining a stronger sense of who I am allows me to place my energy in the right direction. I am letting my ego thaw from a victim complex. I am a whole person, and there is no other person like me in the world. Don't you believe the same can be true for you? I am a person with depression and anxiety; not someone with a disorder. Don't get me wrong, I have days when my mind does not work. By relying on my recovery, I use the tools I have been taught to get through difficult times. During dark moments I am learning the best thing to do is to radically accept my feelings—knowing they will not continue forever.

My purpose in writing this book is to allow me to serve you and those close to you. This work has transformed me as I let go of bitterness and anger toward those who hurt me. Therefore, by reading this piece of nonfiction, you are serving yourself and those you care about. Recovery teaches us that taking care of ourselves is not optional—it is imperative. Picking up this text and reading it is one way to take care of yourself.

At this point, my life is more peaceful. I feel what I want in my life will happen, and change is possible. I will continue using the tools I have been given to manage my mind, emotions, and body, and I will remain fit as a fiddle. I am relinquishing the grip of depression, anxiety, and trauma, which is not easy to do but is necessary if I want to be free.

You may be asking yourself, what does my recovery look like? The not-complex answer is managing my physical, mental, and emotional well-being. I follow a daily routine, take supplements and prescriptions, eat right, exercise, enjoy time with my wife and children, spend time with Dad, write, and schedule social activities such as having coffee with a friend or tackling a puzzle with my wife. Recovery activities provide meaning and purpose for me.

My relationship with God allows me to succeed in accomplishing His will for me and having faith in Him. I attend therapy sessions approximately one time a month. I go whether I require it or my symptoms are in remission. Going is like having a massage each month regardless of whether I have back pain or none at all. This habit prevents knots from forming beginning at the nape of the neck to the end of my spine. I have ongoing communication with a psychiatrist about my mood. He will adjust my cocktail of medicines when necessary. I attend two support groups each week. I took the initiative to start one of these groups using Zoom. My aim in life is to utilize my life experiences to serve others with mental health conditions. In 2019, I became a Certified Peer Specialist (CPS) in the state of Wisconsin. A CPS advances activities and actions that help improve or enhance a peer's strengths and their ability to cope with the strain of daily life and is a person with lived experience of having a mental health condition or addiction.

Whatever the reason you selected to read my story, I hope it may assist you or others with ideas for your own recovery pathway. I want it to change your and others' attitudes, assumptions, and ideas about mental health and addictions.

Whenever a recoveree requests me to join their journey, I feel blessed. With that said, those asking for help must be ready to let go of their old self and embrace a new life of hope, healing, and health.

NOTES

1. You are welcome to join my virtual Peer Recovery Support Group on Thursday evenings. The information about the group and how to join is in the appendix of this book.
2. Substance Abuse and Mental Health Services Association (SAMHSA) Brochure, "Working Definition of Recovery: Ten Guiding Principles" (Printed 2012).

REFLECTION

What have I learned from reading this chapter?

CHAPTER 2

STARTING LINE-UP

Childhood Development

If I could wake up tomorrow morning without depression and anxiety, this is what it looks like: The automatic negative thinking would turn into positive, empowering thoughts; a cloud of sadness that lingers in my soul would become a sunny, blue sky; my irritable mood would become light and flexible, and I would experience joy in my life.

The moment I realized I had a serious condition, I was thirty years old and interviewing a girl who was abused by a parent. She described in detail her experience of sexual and emotional abuse, which caused an emotional trigger for me. An image flashed in my mind of the physical and emotional abuse I suffered from as a child by my parents. Emotions began flooding my brain like a river overflowing its banks. Returning home from work that evening, I was frozen and in a fog because of the overwhelming fear and anxiety I felt.

The next day at work, a coworker said to me, "You don't look well. Is there someone you can speak to about this recent experience?" I was resistant to the idea because I was a social worker. I believed, "Therapy is for *those* people." However, I knew then that I needed to talk to someone about what happened.

I attended my first therapy session reluctant to talk about my problem. I described in detail my childhood and early adult experiences. The therapist said, "You may be experiencing clinical depression and anxiety based on the symptoms you are sharing with me. I would like to make a referral to a psychiatrist to determine if medication may be helpful. Are you willing to make an appointment?"

I was familiar with psychiatry because my mom was seeing a psychiatrist for her diagnosis of bipolar disorder, and I learned about it during my social work training. I could not think clearly or focus, and my stomach tossed and turned like shaking a can of peas. I realized something was not right within me. I became determined to figure out what was causing my emotional storm and made an appointment to see a psychiatrist to address my symptoms. In order to understand the present, sometimes it is necessary to look into the past.

When the time came for me to be born, my dad was sent to the waiting area sitting on pins and needles praying everything was going to be fine. Dad recalls the nurse saying, "Please remain in the lounge area. It is hospital policy that you cannot be present in the birthing room area."

When Dad returned to Mom's hospital room, he could see she was totally spent on the birthing process. When I consider the sacrifice, pain, and subsequent joy of her giving birth to me, it is truly a miraculous event.

Dad realized he had a son, and informed relatives and friends of my birth. He was able to view me from the nursery window. He awaited the moment when he could hold me in his arms for the first time. He noticed Mom looking sad—she was withdrawn and clenched her fists as if holding on for dear life. Dad said, "Do you want to hold our son?" Mom responded, "Not right now." At that moment it became painfully clear to Dad that something was not right with Mom.

Mom's father had two brothers who made an effort to see me in the hospital. The brothers had a reputation for being obnoxious. On the drive to the hospital, they made a few pit stops to enjoy an adult beverage or two. When they entered the hospital room, Dad smelled alcohol on their breaths as they were greeting Mom. The brother that was bald and had very red cheeks, calloused hands, and a potbelly, with a twinkle in his eye said to Mom, "Margaret, we are here to see the snowbank." My parents were unsure why he made such a claim. Later Dad realized it was a connection to our last name, Winter.

In my baby book, Mom wrote that I had blue eyes, black hair, a fair complexion, and a funny little nose. She thought I had the features of her dad, my grandfather. Several relatives and friends brought gifts to Mom and Dad. Most of the gifts were practical items such as a crib, pajamas, a play-set, pants, a shirt, a blanket, and money.

After my birth, Dad noticed Mom's mood was low, and she struggled with being a new mom. Feeding, changing diapers, and meeting my other needs were difficult for her. She became overwhelmed when I needed care. The burden of meeting my needs fell on Dad.

A cloud began to form over the Winter residence. Mental health conditions, especially bipolar disorder were not widely understood in the sixties; in fact, people with these conditions were marginalized by society. We lived in a small, rural community where the attitude was, "You just need to pull yourself up by the bootstraps."

Initially, Dad was blamed by the family for her condition, like he was a puppet master that controlled her every move. Years passed before society and our entire family began to educate themselves about mental health and realize that mental illnesses are biological conditions. Eventually, the family came to the epiphany that Dad was not the cause of Mom's condition. Dad shared, "I was under a tremendous amount of stress balancing work, Mom's health, and being a parent."

I needed nurturing to feel safe and develop an emotional bond with my mom. I do not believe Mom and I were able to emotionally attach due to her mental health condition. Sometime during my first year of life, Mom was hospitalized in the psychiatric ward for fourteen days in an effort to stabilize her mood. Dad said, "Mom struggled to understand what was going on inside of her."

My guess is she experienced an inability to control her mood, which caused panic. I question whether she felt anything when she looked at me or if her condition caused her to emotionally withdraw and check out. If so, this left an emotional hole inside of me. Relatives offered to fill my emotional needs. However, even now, making an emotional connection with people is very difficult for me. I suspect this was due to the lost opportunity I experienced as a baby to make an emotional connection with Mom. I do not blame her for this since her mental health was a disease of the brain, which affected her ability to function normally, and robbed her of happiness.

In the course of my first year of a new life, I began to grow. I was like a butterfly that underwent a metamorphosis during its life cycle. The early stage is called the larval, when it is a caterpillar, until the final stage when it becomes a beautiful and graceful young butterfly. Like the butterfly, I began to sit up, take my first step, and walk. I said my first words, "All done," and I was very fond of bananas. Mom recorded these firsts in a baby diary she kept for me because, despite her illness, she wanted to record these major events. Although she tried, Mom's condition caused her to miss several firsts in my life.

I spent the first Christmas with my paternal grandparents. Mom documented in my baby book when I was four months old that I was growing into a handsome blond, weighed 18 pounds 13 ounces, and was 27 ½ inches tall. Once my first birthday arrived, Mom wrote in my baby diary again, "Larry is 32 inches in length, weighed 25 pounds, and

13 ounces." My first tooth appeared on January 1, 1965; the second tooth became visible on January 28; and by April 18, 1965, the seventh tooth peeked through my gums. My first birthday bash was a celebration with relatives. I received several gifts such as a jacket, a workbench, and a telephone. Mom was present but, due to her condition, it continued to be difficult for her to enjoy a moment like this with me. Despite her illness, she started the tradition of making me a German chocolate cake for each subsequent birthday bash. The frosting was the best part of the cake, which included pieces of coconut, pecans, egg yolk, sugar, evaporated milk, and vanilla. Our German heritage made this type of cake a legend in our family, despite the fact, that its origin had nothing to do with our heritage.[1]

Mom was unable to place me in a stroller with a hood over my head to block the sunlight from my face and roll me to the park to share baby stories with other parents. Thinking about this brings tears to my eyes because my heart feels a heavy loss. She was unable to enjoy these simple pleasures with me. Even now, I feel a lump in my throat mourning at this lost opportunity to bond and be connected to her. When I was in distress, she was rarely available to soothe and calm me. I think of a young puppy who yelps to draw attention to itself, and the owner picks the puppy up and cuddles to help their pet calm down. What happens to a puppy neglected by its owner? The puppy may become an adult dog that refuses to submit to the demands of its owner, cuddle, or be playful. The dog may become mean toward other people. This is similar to how an unattached baby may behave in its adult years. The inability to bond with Mom caused me to believe I was unimportant, defective, and not worthy of nurturing. Dad tried nobly to fill the void in Mom's absences. He relied on his mother and sister to provide nurturing and companionship for me.

I feel sad for Mom because she was unable to enjoy the special moments in my life. When I was in my early fifties, she expressed regret for missing these special events. When she told me this, there was no emotion on her part. Did she feel anything for me as a child, or was she simply numb? I am curious to know how family members interacted with me during my first year of life. Unfortunately, those family members I could ask are now deceased. Certainly, I kept them busy with feeding and changing diapers. Dad said, "You were bottle-fed, because of Mom's condition."

A photograph taken by Dad on my second Christmas showed I wore red pants held up by red suspenders, a white long-sleeved tee-shirt, and a pair of white ankle-high shoes. Because Mom experienced a bipolar attack, it fell to Dad and my paternal grandma and grandpa Winter to make the day joyful. A picture of me was taken showing the decorated tree with silver tinsel, red ornaments, and white lights.

Prior to my third Christmas, I became quite ill. The tree was already up and decorated in the living room of our home when I was hospitalized with a very high temperature and suffered from dehydration. Dad told me later, "You were burning up."

I was given a toy car by my parents for the third Christmas. The car had a black steering wheel and a white seat I could sit in. It was made of metal, and the exterior of the car was white with a red stripe on the side. I used my feet to make it go forward, backward, or sideways. Today there is something similar called a big wheel, made mostly of plastic, that moves by placing feet on the peddles to turn the wheels. Before I returned home from the hospital, Dad got rid of the car. He said, "I just could not stomach seeing it because it brought back memories of you and we thought you would die."

He remained in the hospital with me for four days without leaving my side as a virus attacked my body. I remained in the hospital bed, lifeless, pale, and on the edge of death. A small incision was made inside my right ankle bone about an inch in diameter, which housed the IV needle to feed me. A steady dose of a solution was delivered into my body. The scar is visible today and appears similar to the dimensions of an eyebrow. Dad said, "Mom visited when she caught the occasional ride to the hospital with a member of the family." I was a fighter during my illness, eventually coming home to finish my recovery without any further complications.

I am curious about what it must have been like for her to feel emotionally distant from her own child. My emotional connection to my mom was absent because she did not hold me or take care of my needs for the first three years of my life. Dad told me, "When you were an infant, you had a difficult time falling asleep; the only way I could calm you down was by laying you on my bare chest. This reduced your anxiety, soothed you, and helped with other feelings you may have been experiencing."

As an adult, I feel a sense of loss that my mom was emotionally unavailable to me. The lack of attachment to her had an impact on me later in my life, which I will go into detail about later in the book.[2]

As I mentioned, my family grew up in a small, rural community where people cared about the well-being of one another, but according to Dad, some of Mom's family and friends found it difficult to understand her condition. In the fifties, sixties, and seventies, it was common to believe that struggling with mental health was a moral shortcoming. Her parents sought care for her condition, but in those years, little was known about how to treat her symptoms. Mom said, "A doctor prescribed Valium to ease the tension in my mind."

Valium was a common drug back then used to treat anxiety. She felt anxious most of the time. Her feelings were similar to my experience with anxiety, like a volt of electricity traveling daily throughout her body. She coped with anxiety during her adolescence by smoking with her girlfriends. Likely it offered her a chemical to settle her anxious mind and body.

Mom was an anxious child, her condition was worsened by her parents, specifically her mother. She shared a story with me about the physical abuse she suffered at the hands of her own mother. Grandma used a wooden spoon to punish Mom, which she described as "a horrendous experience," which locked into her memory for the remainder of her life. Grandma suffered an apparent heart attack during my mom's teenage years. The family had so little regard for my mom that they forced her to become a care-taker for Grandma. Mom was the cook and cleaner. She washed and dried clothes and did other domestic duties while Grandma recovered. There were times when Mom was pulled out of school to be the caretaker. Grandpa was the owner of a tavern-supper club combination, spending up to sixteen hours a day tending to his business.

Mom's emotional needs went unmet because she was the caretaker for Grandma during Grandpa's absences. Grandpa stood 6 feet 2 inches tall, wore glasses, had big hands, had a slender build, and looked like Abraham Lincoln without a beard. Grandpa and Grandma lived next to the business. This allowed Grandpa to be near Grandma in the event of an emergency. Grandpa was compassionate toward others, giving of his time, talent, and treasure. He was the chief of the fire department and president of the school board. Mom states, "He was a good man in the eyes of members of the community, but there was also a dark side to him. He was an alcoholic, had an affair with another woman, and he had drinks at both ends of the bar while bartending."

Mom's childhood abuse caused seeds of shame to wreak havoc in her mind and heart. She believed, "I'm bad." She repeated this mantra up until her death. She became con-ditioned not to share her feelings, do everything she could to please Grandma, and be seen but not heard. Grandma expected Mom to take care of her.

In Mom's early twenties, she began receiving psychiatric care, which continued until her death on June 19, 2021. Mom was hospitalized several times for mental health episodes in her late twenties and thirties. Dad said, "Mom went through three to five shock treatments (Electroconvulsive therapy ECT), and I noticed a slight improvement but the effects did not last long."[3] Eventually, the doctor placed her on Lithium. Lithium was one of the first drugs manufactured to treat bipolar, psychosis, and depression. The medicine stabilized her most of the time to avoid the need for longer-term hospitalization.

As an adult, I had several conversations with Mom, and she continued to believe she did something bad to cause her condition. The doctor attempted many times to help her understand that bipolar is due to her brain's inability to produce chemicals that directly relate to mood, motivation, and thinking. She had severe episodes of depression and mania, which were manifested by extreme highs and lows in her mood. I cannot imagine the loneliness, isolation, and pain she endured throughout her lifetime.

Mom began to share her childhood experiences with me in her seventies. When she spoke about her childhood, her lower lip quivered, her tone of voice was bitter, and she exhibited an awareness of the impact the circus atmosphere of her childhood had on her adult behavior.

Grandma had a solid frame, wore cat-eye glasses, and was always in a dress. She had an affinity for wearing the same dress every day. She grew up during the deep depression era when the essentials of daily life were scarce and finances were tight. Although the Great Depression ended in the late forties, she continued to act like the Depression was still alive in the seventies. In her pantry, she had large plastic bags filled with bread ties that no doubt she had saved for years. One time I said to her, "Grandma, why do you keep those white things in the bags"? She replied, "Larry, you never know when I or someone may need one."

I had a normal relationship with Grandma. During childhood, I enjoyed conversations with her, and she gave me her attention when we were together. Occasionally I remained overnight when my parents were away for an evening or went on vacation. I remember waking to the smell of eggs, toast, and sometimes oatmeal. My favorite breakfast was her poached eggs. She left the yolks soft so that I could take a piece of toast and prick the yolk. When I finished breakfast on a school day, I gathered my books and skipped out the door toward school, which was about a block from Grandma's home. She was always willing to bake for family gatherings, and she often mended socks and sewed pants for our family. She never raised her voice at me, nor did she ever hit me. I'm left with only fond memories of her.

Based on what I saw with interactions between Grandma and Mom, they seemed normal together. In fact, when she described her abusive childhood, I was shocked to think Grandma was capable of being abusive toward her. Overtly there was no evidence of bitterness or anger from Mom toward Grandma. It was not until she was in her seventies that she expressed her feelings of displeasure toward Grandma, who by this time had already been dead for several years. She had a sister and brother who were much older than she was. Once they became adults, they left home during her adolescence. They offered no protection from Grandma.

When mom was eighteen, she went on a date with a man who was known for getting around. She was a virgin, which was a value she held dearly as a Catholic woman. The man smooth-talked and attempted to have his way with her. She resisted his advances to "get in her pants," as she described it. The man hoped to break Mom's spirit so that he could have sex with her. When she told this story, I could see in her eyes and tell by the tone of her voice the amount of trauma this incident caused her.

Mom had four girlfriends as a youth. Despite these friends not understanding her condition, they were an important part of her entire life. They were wild about Elvis Presley, the king of rock and roll. Many parents during his era were appalled at the way he behaved. His hips did pumps and thrusts as if he was circling a hula hoop. Some people believed he was the devil incarnate. Her band of girlfriends called themselves the "Hound Dogs." The group of five women remained close friends for more than seventy years and got together with their spouses to play cards one time per month. They celebrated each other's birthdays and anniversaries, went camping with their families together, went on vacations, and did other special activities together.

NOTES

1. Foodicles, "German Chocolate Cake History: From Germany?" (Printed January 26, 2021).
2. B. A. Van der Kolk, *The Body Keeps the Score* (Penguin Books 2014): 113.
3. Electroconvulsive Therapy, Cleveland Ohio medical clinic, (May 13, 2014): https://my.clevelandclinic.org/health/treatments/9302-electroconvulsive -therapy.

REFLECTION

What have I learned from reading this chapter?

CHAPTER 3

TURNOVERS

Parental Miscues

While I was in elementary school, things continued to change in the Winter household. When I did something wrong, Dad became violent and hit me with his belt. Dad was 5 feet 10 inches tall, wore glasses, and had an athletic-looking appearance. When I heard the sound of a slap from a belt in his hands it was like a thunderstorm, signaling justice was about to be served. He would forcibly yank down my pants and underwear and delivered several painful blows to my backside with his leather belt. The blows made a sound similar to a trainer whipping a horse. *Whack! Whack!*

In elementary school, I broke my wrist at a Cub Scouts event. There was a steep hill in front of the building. My friends and I thought it would be fun to roll down the hill. I was about halfway down and I rolled over my right wrist. Suddenly I heard a *Crack!* I knew something happened. I was taken to the emergency room and an X-ray confirmed

I fractured my wrist. Shortly after the cast was removed, I was undressing for my bath. Dad approached me, visibly upset about something I did that I cannot recall. Totally unexpectedly, he grasped my wrist in his hand and threw me into the bathtub. Horrified by that, Mom pushed her way into the bathroom and put herself between us. I peered at my wrist; it was red in several different spots. I was shaken, scared that he might become violent toward Mom. Instead, Dad's rage continued to be directed at me, he called me "a little shit" and other words that pierced my heart.

His rage escalated at other times when my behavior was not according to his expectations, or I misbehaved. Like any child, I did things that were wrong that warranted discipline. However, the severity of Dad's verbal and physical abuse came at a high emotional cost to my development. I internalized his discipline because I believed I was a "Bad Boy" and didn't deserve to receive love, and I stuffed my feelings inside.

Between the ages of six and twelve, my awareness of feelings wilted away year by year. When disciplined, I would lay on my belly, pants pulled down, and wait for the deliberate blows to my backside to begin. I squirmed like a worm in an effort to avoid the impact of these lashings. Tears would slide down my cheeks and drip onto the carpet in our home. I would scream at the top of my lungs for Dad to stop this horrific abuse of my body and soul. The louder I cried, the harder I would be beaten. By the time I was twelve, feelings of pain, despair, anger, fear, and sadness were no longer available to me. I felt numb due to the years of abuse suffered at the hands of Mom and, to a greater extent, by Dad.

A coping skill I used was detaching my mind from my body. This is a mental process of disconnecting from my thoughts, feelings, memories, or sense of identity. I disconnected from myself and had problems dealing with difficult emotions.[1] I remained in my head to avoid feeling the pain of the lashings administered by my dad. Detaching reduced the intensity of my pain. My history of maltreatment can be linked to my current physical, psychological, and behavioral struggles. I suffer from a gastrointestinal disorder, osteoporosis, depression, anxiety, and trauma.[2]

As a child, I suppose I could have ended the abuse by telling a doctor, teacher, clergy, or some other person in authority who had the power to intervene. Protecting myself never crossed my mind as an option. I wondered, "If I told another person, would Dad become even crueler toward me?"

I urge any child who is being physically abused to tell an authority figure immediately. I urge any adult who discovers a child is being physically hurt to report the abuse to your local Department of Child Protection Services. I realize telling another person is frightening. However, every human being has the right to be treated with love, care, and compassion regardless of the behavior that causes this primitive response of physical harm toward you or another person. During my childhood, I began noticing that my dad's discipline was different from the practice of other dads. Friends made poor choices but did not receive physical punishment for their behavior. Sometimes when I went to a friend's home to play, they responded, "I am grounded," or they might have their bike privileges suspended.

At family gatherings, I played with my cousins. Mom's brother and sister had children similar in age to me. We were known as the "Three Musketeers." As cousins, we had a close relationship with each other and often became involved in roughhousing. Our behavior would lead to breaking things or getting into minor scuffles over games we played. When our parents investigated who was guilty of their actions, often the finger was pointed toward me. When this occurred, Dad's eyes would become wide like a saucer, his mouth open, and the tips of his ears beet red. He would come after me like an angry pit bull, ready to attack another person. With an open hand, he would slap my face or whack another part of my body.

Dad's actions embarrassed me. Most of these events were not my fault, but my cousins pointed at me because they learned from past experience that Dad would immediately pounce on me and ask questions later. I felt humiliated in front of my relatives. I never attempted to defend myself. If I had, I feared Dad would perceive this as an act of rebellion and cause further pain to me.

Relatives gathered one evening at our home. I listened as my relatives shared stories, gossiped, and reminisced about some crazy activities they did when they were younger. I hung on to each word and recorded what was shared in my memory. My uncle was in his teens when I was seven or eight years old. He was someone I looked up to. He and I enjoyed playing together despite our age difference. Of course, sometimes we were a little rough with each other. In our living room, there were two pink flamingos. The flamingos sat in an upright position; they had beady little black eyes and were located in a corner of the living room on top of a light gray wool carpet.

My uncle and I wrestled with each other, akin to David who fought Goliath. My uncle said, "I am going to take you down." I was much smaller in stature than he was. He backed into one of the flamingos on our living room floor and cracked the upper portion of the flamingo's chest. "Oh-oh, we are going to be in trouble for our actions from my dad." I positioned the broken flamingo behind my back in an effort to make it go unnoticed. The relatives decided to migrate from the kitchen area into the living room.

Dad entered the living room, stopped dead in his tracks, and immediately noticed my body position in front of the flamingo. "What are you hiding, Larry?" My heart began to beat hard, my cheeks turned red, and I avoided direct eye contact with my dad. He stepped toward me, looked at me, then at the broken flamingo, and realized one of the flamingos had a crack in its chest. He said, "What the hell happened here? Who did this?" My uncle sat two feet from the flamingo and pointed his finger directly toward me. I said, "I didn't do it." Before I said anything. Dad was noticeably pissed. He raised his open hand and smacked me across the face. Then, he grabbed my right arm and pushed me away from the flamingo in order to get a proper view of the crack. I said, "But, Dad, Uncle is the one who broke it, not me."

It made little difference, Dad had already played his part as judge, juror, and prosecutor.

Relatives were stunned by his outburst. No one came to my defense or intervened to halt Dad's anger. I felt humiliated because it was done in front of relatives. I thought I was a bad person despite being innocent of any wrongdoing.

Most of the physical abuse stopped when I was twelve. One day I heard Mom say to Dad, "He is getting too big for the belt lashings." Dad had a difficult time placing me in a face-down position, pulling my pants and underwear down, and holding me.

By this time in life, I felt a huge amount of anger toward my parents but kept it inside. I once heard, "Anger turned inward becomes depression." I believe this statement speaks to my experience. I continue to be reluctant to show my anger, fearing I may become out of control like Dad.

There were a few episodes as a young adult when my dad physically assaulted me. After sophomore year in college in the late summer, a girlfriend and I went to a campground my parents were vacationing at. I don't recall the reason Dad was angry with me, but I do remember being slapped alongside my head. I grabbed the arm of my girlfriend, walked quickly to the car, jumped into the vehicle, started the engine, backed up, and drove to my girlfriend's home. My aunt and uncle were present during this episode. My aunt told me that my uncle said to my dad, "You are going to cause Larry to eventually resent you because of the way you treat him."

On another occasion during my junior year in college, my parents attended homecoming weekend to watch me play in a basketball game. I asked a woman to accompany me on a date. I was so excited about dating someone after a year without a close female friend. A group of friends and I made a reservation to dine at a local restaurant after the game. We did not invite parents to dine with us so that we could be free to be obnoxious and raise a little hell. My parents went to a local bar, not too far from the campus. I let them know I would meet them later that evening.

My date was a beautiful woman with brown hair and smooth, silky skin. Typically, after a game, I was famished due to running up and down a basketball court for an hour and thirty minutes. We joined a few classmates, team members, and their girlfriends at the restaurant to feast on barbecue chicken, baked potato, soft rolls, and vegetables. After the meal, we went back to the campus for the homecoming dance.

When we no longer wanted to stay at the dance, my date and I decided to join my parents in their hotel room. I stopped at a gas station to pick up a six-pack of beer to share with them. Previously, I had asked my date if she would like to meet my parents. She was open to the idea and looked forward to meeting them. I knocked on their hotel room door a few times, waiting until Dad opened the door. Immediately, I realized something was wrong. Mom was in bed on her side, her back facing us, and she was crying. When I looked into Dad's bloodshot eyes, I noticed he was drunk. Immediately, I became scared as hell because I knew alcohol had the capacity for him to become violent toward me.

He said, "We came all this way to see you, and you are spending no time with us." As I looked into his eyes, I felt afraid of what he might do to me. I reminded Dad about our conversation prior to their arrival. I planned to spend most of my time with friends after the completion of the basketball game. Mom cried even louder like a child having a temper tantrum.

Without warning, Dad smacked me across the face. Dad's anger boiled. He said, "You little shit."

I looked at the face of my date; she gasped with horror. Dropping the six-pack of beer on the floor, I grabbed my date's sleeve and abruptly left the room. We walked quickly, entered the elevator, and selected the lobby floor button. We left the hotel lobby and looked back to the entrance to see if Dad might follow us. I fumbled to find the right key as we approached my car door. I quickly unlocked the car door and looked back again to see if Dad had followed us. Fortunately, he had not. We drove out of the hotel lot and went to join our friends at a party. We were both shaken by the events, so I proceeded to drink heavily in an attempt to forget the whole ordeal.

When I awoke the next morning, I had a violent headache and dry mouth, and my stomach did flip flops like it does when I'm riding a roller coaster. Despite a hangover, I agreed to meet Mom and Dad for breakfast. I arrived at the hotel, and they had already checked out of their room and were waiting for me in their vehicle. I approached the vehicle, looked into a window on the passenger's side, and noticed Dad was curled up in a ball in the back seat with a massive hangover. When I opened the vehicle door, he began to cry. Dad felt guilty when he hit me in the face in the hotel room. He said, "I am sorry; I should have not done that."

When I was fifty-six years old and my dad was eighty-two, I felt safe and comfortable asking him how he was treated as a boy by my grandfather, his dad. During Dad's childhood, he experienced harsh discipline from my grandfather and later transmitted it to me. Dad said, "I got hit with an object, most of the time I deserved it since I could be a little shit." A well-known author on spiritual matters, Father Richard Rohr states, *"If we do not transform our pain, we will most assuredly transmit it—usually to those closest to us: our family, our neighbors, our coworkers, and, invariably, the most vulnerable, our children."*[3]

I take my emotional pain out on myself rather than hurting others. Generally, people who suffer from abuse develop coping strategies to get through a day such as drinking, drugs, gambling, obsessive-compulsive behavior like hoarding, and others. I used food to soothe myself.

Middle school was three blocks from home. Because I was close to home I could walk to school and come home during lunchtime. Dad worked the second shift at a manufacturing plant, which prevented me from seeing him after school and before bedtime. As a family, we ate the biggest meal of the day at lunchtime due to Dad's work schedule.

Usually, I ate quickly so that I could get back to school during recess time and play basketball, kickball, football, or softball. Along the school route was a tavern that sold candy. I used paper route earnings to buy candy bars. Usually, it was more than one. Immediately after I purchased the bars, I exited the tavern quickly because I detested the smell of stale beer and cigarettes.

Walking on the sidewalk to school, I would rip the wrapper off the first bar and devour the bar as if it was my last meal. The chocolate and caramel filling was a favorite of mine, smooth and creamy. Next, I would unwrap the second bar and devour it too. Like a monkey gorging on bananas, I would stuff my stomach to the point I would feel ready to explode. I felt self-conscious about allowing people to see me feasting on candy bars. By the time I arrived at school, I made sure there was no evidence of my indulgence. However, I felt a lot of guilt and shame for my actions. I remember thinking, "I am going to gain weight and become the Goodyear blimp."

In addition to my candy bar ritual at lunchtime, I often ate a large turtle sundae when I returned home from school, which caused me to steadily gain weight. I was a participant on the fifth-grade basketball team. After practice one night, my coach approached Mom and said, "Stop feeding him all those pork chops." I was deeply hurt by the coach's comment. I began to believe I was less than adequate, and that there was no doubt I would become like Porky Pig. From this moment forward, I developed an unhealthy relationship with food that continues to impact me today.

The abuse and unhealthy coping strategies were instrumentally averse to my growth and development, causing me to whittle away at my identity. Mom's bipolar illness, Dad's physical abuse, coping with my relationship with food, and basketball achievements, created a false sense of who I really was.

During adulthood when I spoke about my childhood abuse, I felt sadistically alive. Depression and anxiety were forces that gave me meaning and purpose similar to a career. I realize that my view of myself and reality are shaped differently than many people due to my mom's condition and the physical abuse I was subjected to by my dad. I believed, "Something must be wrong with me." Unless I was being treated abusively or in another emotionally harmful way, I failed to feel normal. I was drawn to people who hurt me. When I was around "nice" people, I found them to be soft, weak, and boring. In a wayward way, the abuse transformed into a sadistic pleasure for me.

Fortunately for me, the incident in the hotel room was the final time I was hit by Dad. Despite this incident, my date from that night and I went out again and continued to do so for three more years. I was surprised she went on another date with me. I guess she wanted to be with me because I was a star basketball player and good-looking.

There are moments when I am mentally and emotionally stuck. At these times, I find it difficult to extinguish the memories of physical and emotional abuse. Sometimes I think back to my childhood to reflect on what it was like to be a victim of abuse. Therefore, until I was fifty-one years old, my view of the world was polluted by the past. Throughout adulthood, I kept visits at home with my parents to a minimum. My body was on high alert in order to be ready to protect myself if my parents lashed out at me. This continued into my forties.

When I would return home after a visit with my parents, I would be emotionally exhausted. The knot in my stomach and tension in my muscles would take time to dissolve before I could regain a healthy state of mind. In between, I did not treat myself well. I would say to myself, "I need to be a better son." I excessively exercised, over-controlled my food intake, and ignored the pain inside me. Unfortunately, this cycle went on for many years. It took a long time for me to be able to understand the impact trauma had on my body and mind.

It is difficult to filter information when my depression and anxiety worsen. I cope by developing tunnel vision and hyperfocus. For me, hyperfocus is a deep concentration, tuning everything else out. It is detrimental to ongoing relationships, but it can also be positive, as evidenced by many scientists, artists, and writers.[4] Career success is where I displayed my hyperfocus. This left little time for recreation, pleasure, and close relationships. When I could not shut down, I would block out the world around me through isolation and exercise. I constantly fought trauma, which left me exhausted, fatigued, and depressed. Sadness became my primary emotion, and hiding the truth about childhood experiences became my primary preoccupation.

NOTES

1. https://www.betterhealth.vic.gov.au/health/conditionsandtreatments/diss ociation-and-dissociative-disorders#bhc-content; Department of Health, State of Victoria Australia, "Dissociation and Dissociative Disorders": Copyright State of Victoria Australia 20212.
2. Rossen, Hudley, Cicchetti, Rogodsch, "Long Term Consequences of Child Abuse and Neglect," Fact sheet Child Welfare Information Gateway (April 2019); https://www.childwelfare.gov/pubs/factsheets/long-term-consequences.
3. B. Johnson, "Spiritual Speaking: It is best to embrace our wounds, not ignore" (SWnews media November 4, 2018); https://www.swnewsmedia. com/eden_prairie_news/news/opinion/columnists/spiritually-speaking-it-is -best-to-embrace-our-wounds-not-ignore/article_cbce3444-85f2-5f54- 915c-2e3f627d60c1.html.
4. Healthline by Eloise Porter. Updated February 19, 2019.

REFLECTION

What have I learned from reading this chapter?

PART TWO

BE IMPERFECT

CHAPTER 4

BENCHED

Healing the Shame that Binds Me

Shame is manufactured throughout my entire family. Shame focuses on me, like, "I *am* bad," and guilt focuses on behavior, as in, "I *did* something bad." Shame is a part of bullying, addiction, depression, anxiety, and other behaviors. Mom strived to be perfect, always be liked, and never let people see the emotional turmoil she was in. When Mom fell short in these areas, she believed, "I am bad," or "I sinned." In the public's eye, Dad practiced emotional control, did not want to be perceived as weak, made work and status his primary objective, and was prone to violence. In my family, there was a petri dish of secrecy, silence, and judgment. As a result of these factors, I internalized shame.

I have several memories of shame from childhood. One evening at sunset, Mom and I were looking out our living room window with a view of the front yard. The window cranked open on either side. Mom stood directly in front of the window gazing out into the yard. Suddenly she became excited, shouting, "There goes Uncle Harold with a ladder on top of his car!"

Uncle Harold was Mom's brother. I looked out the window and saw absolutely nothing. Mom's comment disturbed me. I gently said, "Mom there is nothing going by." Mom threw up her hands and bellowed at the top of her lungs, "That is Uncle Harold's car with a ladder on top; don't you see it?"

Our eyes made contact with each other. Mom appeared withdrawn like she was in a different universe. All I could see was the street in front of our house and, beyond that, a creek. This image energized her and made her manic. The emotional high gave her the energy of an impulsive child. Her frenzied behavior lasted seventy-two hours without sleep. Not yet in kindergarten when this episode occurred, I was frightened by Mom's behavior and had no clue how to help her.

Again I told her there was nothing there, and she shouted, "It's there; can't you see it?" I thought I had said something wrong and I was crazy. Now I realize I was a child with an inability to step back and look at the situation for what it was. Repeated occurrences like this caused me to shame myself and believe I was responsible for Mom's unusual behavior. Finally, around age fifty-one, I began to realize I needed to detach from Mom and not take on her shame. Mom had eighteen mental health breakdowns during the course of her life that led to hospitalizations. Her unresolved shame played a major role in those hospitalizations.

When Mom was seventy-eight years old, she called me from the Assisted Living Facility. It had been a decade since her last hallucination. She said, "When I was a youth, I was prescribed tranquilizers and Valium." When she spoke, her voice was crisp and harsh. Due to my depression and anxiety, I had a difficult time listening to her speak.

Suddenly, a voice in my head said, "You are bad."

During childhood, I often experienced shame when a situation like this occurred. I am hopeful this voice will continue to decrease through my participation in support groups, regularly seeing a therapist and a psychiatrist, and nurturing relationships with others.

Shame motivated me to become an overachiever in an attempt to quash shameful thoughts running through my heart and soul. I reasoned that achievement demonstrates, "I am a good person." I have since realized shameful thoughts are not true, and I will no longer allow them to define who I am. I still have days when shameful thoughts return. However, as I continue to age and heal, the intensity is less.

Mom spoke about regrets in her life such as not attending college due to her bipolar illness and following her doctor's advice not to bear another child of her own. She often said, "I should have been a nun."

Mom and Dad tried to adopt, but the agency they applied to believed it was not a good idea due to Mom's bipolar condition. She told me she wanted to have a girl, "So that you would not be alone."

Until her death in June of 2021, she continued to comment, "I am bad," "I should go to jail," or "I did something wrong." Shame kept her mind in a prison for most of her life.

It took many years for me to realize the consequences of living in an abusive home and of being raised by a mom who suffered from an unmanaged mental health condition. Physical punishment as a child made me believe when I did something wrong, "I must be bad." The healing work I have completed curbs my brain's appetite to think badly of myself. I did make poor choices as a child and young adult. However, another form of discipline could have been doled out to me, rather than physical lashings and blows to the head. No person deserves to be treated in that manner.

To avoid Dad's anger and avoid exacerbating Mom's condition, I modified my behavior when I was around them. I feared if they lost emotional control, they would take it out on me. I remained alert for danger, I became hyperfocused, I kept to myself, and I tried to be seen but not heard.

I became comfortable with shame, believing that if I were to stay in that mental space, then nothing bad would happen to me. As a child, shame caused me to see the world as a war zone. I told myself, "Shame is a just punishment for my sins." I believed everyone felt the same way when they did something wrong or bad. With time, wisdom, and healing, childhood shame is slowly melting away. I admit I continue to have an emotional connection to shame. However, when shame surfaces in my mind I quickly catch it, extinguish it, and refuse to allow it to direct my behavior.

Although my soul holds my shame, I am adding seeds of compassion, kindness, love, and joy to the weeds of shame. The new seeds kill the weeds of shame, opening a new door to the future for me. I continue to experience shame from time to time as a result of my fallen nature and the world I was born into.

Shame played an integral part in my basketball career. Two coaches reminded me that I was never good enough, despite being one of the best players on the team. During my career, I thought it was normal to be subjected to such scrutiny. The treatment of coaches reinforced what I already believed to be true as a result of my childhood trauma: I would never be good enough. Looking back at my basketball career I realize my identity was defined by my performance, which led me to abuse my body to prove the coaches wrong.

I transferred from the University of Wisconsin–La Crosse (UWL) after my junior year to Viterbo University in La Crosse, Wisconsin, to continue my basketball career. I spent three years at UWL and two years at Viterbo. I was recruited to Viterbo by a previous coach I had at UWL. I had no idea the type of professional career I wanted to pursue. I drank heavily, binged and purged on food, and was severely depressed. One way to purge consisted of exercising and eating Ex-Lax to get rid of food quickly. This pattern of behavior for me dated back to high school.

During my fourth year of college, the basketball season went very well for our team. I pushed myself hard. I received several individual awards such as Academic All-American and tournament Most Valuable Player. I was chosen to play on the small college United States All-Star Team. I was joined by other players from the United States. We played twelve basketball games in New Zealand and Australia. Our team ended with a winning record and several great memories. I felt good about what we accomplished as a team on our tour.

This good feeling did not last long because whenever I accomplished something worthwhile, I allowed shame to bring me down, and I used food to cope. I told myself, "I am not deserving of good feelings because I am bad." I did not allow myself to feel joy or pleasure about the team's success since I did not believe I deserved good fortune in my life.

As a young adult, I noticed the psychological impact my grade school coach had on me when he told my mom, "Stop feeding him pork chops." After his comments, I had become committed to doing whatever it took to get in shape. I was motivated by shame. A daily voice echoed in my head, reminding me I was worthless and fat. I told myself I would defeat the negative voice inside my head.

How did shameful beliefs impact my basketball career? Playing basketball at Viterbo filled my need to exercise, and when I worked out it reduced the negative self-talk, which fed my shame. When I returned to the Viterbo campus from the trip overseas in late May 1987, I yielded to my depression. There were days when it felt like my brain was stuck and in a fog. The only way to overcome being stuck was to exercise. I pushed myself to the point of exhaustion to unblock my brain.

Between my fourth and fifth years of college, our basketball team worked out in the summertime. I pushed myself to remain in shape as the team prepared for the upcoming season, which would be my fifth and final season. During a scrimmage in mid-July, I received a pass from the point guard. I squared my feet toward the basket, which I had done thousands of times, and noticed I had a clear pathway to the goal. Bouncing the ball while my feet charged ahead, I positioned my body to do a layup. I sprung up using my left leg, and my right knee buckled as my right foot returned to the floor. I crumbled to the court, paralyzed by pain. I remember my immediate thought, "This is not going to be good." I hobbled to the training room with assistance from two teammates. I was placed on a training room table, and the trainer examined my condition.

Later that day, the trainer said, "Larry you need medical attention from an orthopedic surgeon."

The doctor conducted a series of tests and diagnosed a right knee anterior cruciate ligament-ACL tear. The ligament runs diagonally in the middle of the knee. It prevents the tibia from sliding out in front of the femur, as well as providing stability to the knee. Fortunately, the doctor informed me, "I am able to repair the damage adequately so that you can finish the final year of your college basketball career. You are going to experience some pain throughout the season, but it will not further damage your knee."

The doctor said, "You will require a knee reconstructive surgery after the completion of the basketball season."

In the fifth year of college, I visited my parents less frequently. When I did return home, the visits were short—usually two days. Thinking about that period of time, I did this to protect my emotional health. I remained alert when I visited them because I did not feel safe at home. Visiting my parents triggered traumatic thoughts, feelings, bitterness, and anger. When I returned to school, I would feel exhausted due to the amount of energy it took to restrain my intense anger and sadness from visiting my parents' home.

I coped with the shame by playing basketball and drinking. When I participated in basketball it released serotonin and dopamine into my brain, which allowed me to focus, study, and play games. When I received a chemical boost, life was manageable for me. However, after a good night's sleep, I faced another day of shame. When I went to sleep at night, I woke up in the morning, and the cycle of shame began again.

I played for a coach who was emotionally abusive and shaming. He said things like, "You are the worst defensive player I have ever coached." I thought this meant I was a bad player. I believed this was a normal way to communicate with athletes.

Dad, in moments of extreme anger and frustration, made statements similar to the coach, like "You are such a klutz." I was drawn to men who were emotionally abusive toward me.

In contrast to many of the men in my life who had treated me poorly, I had an exceptional coach who became a mentor to me. He did not want me purely for my basketball skills but cared deeply for me as a human being. I've always wondered if he intuitively thought I was wounded and in need of healing. He did not have an ego, unlike many coaches that believed they were superior to people. He was a Christian, and his family was a priority despite the demands of his time as a coach. He coached at UWL but continued to take an interest in me when I transferred after my junior year to Viterbo University. Each year, he invited me to have lunch with him to celebrate my birthday. He filled a void in my life as a worthy role model, and I loved him very much. He died on August 23, 2013, at the age of seventy-eight.

In summary, shame is an outcome of the hereditary and harsh treatment I received from my dad. I believed, "There must be something wrong with me; I must be a bad person." The abusive events during my childhood and early adulthood continue to impact my current functioning. To feel safe from trauma and shame, I live in my head. I ignore my body's sensations and feelings as a coping mechanism to avoid emotional pain (although with my efforts to recover, this is changing). I once thought if I allowed myself to feel, I would probably die.

In a journal entry from November 10, 1996, I said "I have a difficult time experiencing pleasure. I believe this stems from the shameful messages I received from my dad and coaches during my childhood. Dad reminded me to not get too big for my 'britches.'"[1] When I strive to do my best, these statements arise in my head from time to time. Due to the messages I received as a child, adolescent, and young adult, shame is a foe I contend with each day. My efforts to recover from shame do not have a grip on my soul like they once had. I dream of the day when I can totally relegate shame to the mental health trash can.

NOTE

1. L. Winter, Journal Entry (November 10, 1996).

REFLECTION

What have I learned from reading this chapter?

CHAPTER 5

TAKING A CHARGE

Sacrificing My Emotions

With a master's degree and no job in March of 1991, I lived on a friend's farm. He generously offered me a living arrangement rent-free until I secured employment. I lived by myself and enjoyed the alone time. He was aware of my depression and anxiety and wanted to relieve me of the burden of paying rent due to being unemployed. Today I continue to be anxious about money despite having adequate financial resources. Why did money impact my emotions? Because Dad was very disturbed about the finances of our family due to mom's mental health. He made it seem as if we were living from paycheck to paycheck. I am conservative with my finances because of this early impression from my childhood. I vowed to never be in a situation of living paycheck to paycheck. Because of my saving habit, an unintentional consequence was the ability to retire from a stressful career in 2018, due to my physical and mental health conditions.

Shortly before I moved to my friend's farm in 1991, a woman I loved broke off our three-year relationship. I was devastated by her decision and decided to fast from dating for a while. She was the first person I dated that I felt an emotional connection. I punished myself with alcohol and stuffed my feelings down to cope with my heartbreak.

Initially, I thought it was depression and anxiety that caused my despair. I knew nothing about trauma at that point in my life. Why did I become sad, fearful, and anxious? I considered several courses of action. Each morning at the farm, I got up feeling very dark and heavy inside but pushed myself to move. I followed a daily routine that consisted of eating breakfast, sitting on the porch to journal, and reading. Next, I would do chores, grocery shop, visit the neighbors, clean the house, or cut the lawn. In the mid-afternoon, I ran or used my exercise bike, which helped manage my depression and anxiety (exercise increases the release of serotonin, a feel-good chemical manufactured in the brain; I was not on medication in 1991). Finally, I prepared dinner and read until bedtime at 10:00 p.m. This routine kept my mind busy, engaged, and temporarily freed me from the darkness inside of me.

During my stay on the farm, money was very tight. Employment was difficult to find after graduation. I was anxious about finding a job and applied for several in the fields of business, social work, and banking. In June of 1991, I received a call to interview for an open social work position in La Crosse County, Wisconsin. The interview went well, and I was offered the position. I had no awareness that my healing journey was about to receive a boost.

I began my social work career in July of 1991, which is when I learned about the impact of childhood trauma on my emotions and behavior. I received no cases for a couple of weeks, mostly due to training.

When I received the first case and my client vividly detailed horrific past abuse, my own stomach became tight. I became extremely anxious, and I had an out-of-body experience. Physically, I was present; mentally, I went somewhere else. Suddenly painful childhood feelings and images flashed into my brain. In one flashback, Dad whipped me with his belt, causing extreme pain and leaving black and blue marks across my buttocks. In another, he came home drunk and stated, "I am proud of you and love you very much." When he said this, it seemed fake because he only said this to me when he had consumed alcohol.

I used food to soothe my emotional distress. In the spring of 1990, I made a decision to enter an outpatient eating disorders program. During the program, I learned the tools to cope with my urges in order to refrain from bingeing and purging. However, the underlying emotional cause went unchecked by the professionals I worked with. I by no means blame them. I assume full responsibility because I was not forthcoming with the treatment team about the extent of my childhood abuse and trauma.

In the nineties, the knowledge and impact of trauma were beginning to make their way into mainstream thinking. I told untruths to myself and failed to open my heart to recover. I continued to battle deep depression and anxiety from 1991 to 1994. In the fall of 1991, a therapist introduced me to a psychiatrist who prescribed fluoxetine (Prozac) to stabilize my mood, but I continued to use food to soothe my emotions.

I became engaged in 1993 to a woman I knew from college. We worked together as social workers in the same Human Service Department in La Crosse, Wisconsin. Due to my depression and anxiety, it was difficult for me to express intimacy with my first wife. She noticed my ongoing struggle with food and wanted to help me. For a second time, I decided to enter a clinic that treated eating disorders. I finally acknowledged the pain from my childhood due to the physical and emotional abuse by my parents. Like a box of chocolates, I never knew what to expect from my parents. Dad's behavior confused me. On one hand, he told me how proud of me he was, and on the other hand, exploded into a violent rage when I made a mistake. I began therapy with a mental health professional that I felt safe with. We worked on the ambivalent feelings I had toward my parents. Also, I began to measure the impact my mom's bipolar condition had on my growth and development as a child, youth, and young adult.

While coming to terms with all of this, I had little time to devote to developing my relationship with my wife. Our interests changed over the time we were together, which caused her to tell me, "We have little in common." She based her worth on external things like having the right type of cell phone, a nice car, clothes, and other material goods. I was learning to understand who I was and what I wanted out of life. I found that I wanted to heal from my childhood experiences and live with a purpose.

Due to both our needs changing, I was committed to working on our marriage. We entered couples counseling and after two sessions my wife said, "I want a divorce". This floored me since I never thought this could happen to me. I told her it was up to her to file for divorce since I wanted to work on healing the issues within our marriage. I remember thinking to myself that I was not going to allow this turn of events to be a reason for a free fall into a deep depression.

We divorced in 2003 after twelve years of marriage. When I was giving testimony in court that I supported the divorce, I recall saying, "I still love you and do not agree with divorcing you. However, because I love you, I will give you the freedom you desire." Once the proceeding ended, I left the courthouse, got in my car, drove away, went to the park, pulled over and began to sob uncontrollably.

In the days that followed, I realized I needed to take time to work on my mental and emotional issues before returning to a committed relationship. I began to believe there is something I am missing, causing me to stay stuck in depression and anxiety.

Fast forward to the springtime of 2015. My mood plummeted for a second time into another deep, dark depression. At the bottom of an emotional abyss, I suffered greatly. This terrified me because I had never experienced this level of darkness before. I was sad, anxious, and unable to work. I had difficulty adding and subtracting, remembering to turn the stove off, and being emotionally present to my family. Heck, I couldn't even balance our checkbook. I felt defeated because I was in and out of therapy for over twenty-five years and continued to end up in the same dark place. Why did these episodes continue despite my efforts to heal?

I went to see a psychologist contracted through my employer's Human Resource Department (HRD). I presented my history to the psychologist because I was ready to open up to someone. My inability to manage my symptoms caused frustration, I felt that I was doing everything right: eating well, exercising, attending therapy, and taking medication. After I told the psychologist about my story, I said to him, "I cannot continue to live this way."

He said, "I believe you are experiencing trauma from your childhood."

Immediately the darkness of my heart began to slowly fade. I could feel a ray of hope seeping its way into my heart. I felt relief wash over me as someone was finally able to understand what was going on with me. I said to myself, "That's it." I began to weep because the psychologist identified exactly what I was missing: trauma's impact on my functioning. It confirmed I was not crazy after all.

Finding help for a mental health condition can be confusing and emotionally overwhelming but help to get started is available. Employees of companies with a Human Resource Department can get information from that office. Your employer has an obligation to provide services, and the provider of the service must keep your conversations confidential, even from your employer. Employees of companies too small to have counseling services or people not employed can find information at a county Health and Human Services department. Most counties have an Aging and Disability Resource Center or similarly named entity that provides free information and guides people to find the support necessary to meet their needs.

Until this point, I managed my trauma by "freezing up" or "numbing out"—escaping into my mind—which was about the best thing I could do. Being physically, mentally, and emotionally immobilized by my trauma permitted me to not feel the harrowing enormity of what was happening to me, which in a hyper-aroused state might threaten my very sanity. In such instances, some of the chemicals I thereby secrete (i.e., endorphins) function as an analgesic, so the pain of injury (to my body or psyche) is experienced with far less intensity. When I binged on food, I fed my trauma, similar to an alcoholic feeding their chemical addiction. I ate massive amounts of food during the day and ignored the signs in my stomach that I was full. When a food binge occurred, I did it in secret.

I prefer being in an environment that is calm and soothing, rather than chaotic and out of control. In large crowds my mind becomes a ping pong ball, moving from overhearing several conversations at one time.

I take prescription medication as an aid to get a good night's rest. Sometimes the nighttime sleep medication does not wear off until late morning, causing drowsiness. When I am writing or typing on my computer, I suddenly catch myself nodding off. When I do consistently get nine to ten hours of sleep each night, it decreases my depression and anxiety.

People have asked me about the efficacy of medication as an aid to stabilize trauma in recovery. I understand the reluctance to take medication. For some, it is about the risk of being labeled. Others allow their pride to get in the way. Some feel a sense of shame due to the way medication is stigmatized in society. Others who may wish to take medication cannot afford the cost. I suggest you seek counsel from a professional and speak to others in your recovery community to learn more about your options.

When I began treatment for trauma at the age of fifty-one, Mom shared her experiences of childhood trauma with me. She described the abuse she suffered at the hands of her mother. Mom's bipolar diagnosis did not mean she was also traumatized. However, several incidents of being hit with a wooden spoon by her mom created trauma for her, which made her bipolar disorder extremely difficult to treat. Trauma occurs to a person by some type of external stimuli rather than just the typical mental health diagnosis that can be associated with hormone deficiencies, a chemical imbalance in the brain, and/or a situational occurrence.

Dad is hesitant to speak about his childhood experiences of abuse by his dad. However, he states, "I could be a little troublemaker." Conventional wisdom believes it is highly likely that the abuser has been abused as a child.

I fear becoming an abuser like Dad. Therefore, I over-compensate by keeping my anger contained. For the last five years, I have been learning to express anger assertively without being aggressive. Anger not processed properly becomes bitterness, which causes physical and emotional turmoil. All the world's religions promote forgiving, which is the simplest, easiest, and quickest way to get rid of anger. This is not letting my abusers off the hook but does allow me to release my anger.

Upon turning fifty-one years old, I realized how horrific my childhood experiences were. It caused me to be hopelessly stuck in the past. The first major step I took to break free from my emotional ties to the past occurred in 1992. I filed a restraining order against my parents, which indicated they were not allowed to have contact with me. The court believed that an accumulation of prior unhealthy incidents was sufficient enough evidence to order my parents to have no contact with me. Before the restraining order, they made several attempts to contact me despite my written pleas to not do so. Looking back, my motivation to have a no-contact order with them was to protect myself from their behaviors and a desire to work with a therapist on the impact my childhood experiences had on my functioning. This separation was extremely difficult for both of us. I spent several holidays alone, feeling lonely and blue without a connection to my family. And Mom and Dad were scared something might happen to me and they may never see me again.

I hung on to the trauma caused in childhood and allowed it to become my identity as an adult.

For many years I white-knuckled my way through life. I suffered from not having contact with my parents. I loved them but did not condone their behavior. I did not deserve to be treated like a lion in a three-ring circus. During childhood, I desperately wanted parents that made me feel loved and protected from mean people in the world. Why did I not feel safe when I was with my parents? The answer is because of their emotional instability.

When I was in sixth grade, Mom and I were in the car together driving around the village we called home. Mom was an Avon Lady selling beauty products mostly to women but also to men. I delivered the merchandise catalogs to Mom's customers so they could purchase the items they wanted. While taking a break from delivering the catalogs, I said to Mom, "I want to attend a seminary and become a priest."

Saint Lawrence Catholic Seminary sat on top of a beautiful hill in a small farming community named, Mount Calvary Wisconsin. The locals called it "God's Country," since several of the villages in the area are named after saints.

I entered the seminary as a freshman. The school had a beautiful chapel made of bricks, a vaulted ceiling, and wood beams. The grounds had several holy statutes, various buildings, and the stations of the cross. On the southeast side of the property, a bowl-shaped softball diamond was dug into the hill, well-groomed with lush green grass. There were three dormitories housing each class, a dining hall not far from the chapel that had several dozen round oak tables able to serve eight to ten students at a time, and a gymnasium located on the south side of the campus. Each class had either a Capuchin priest or brother (a person committed to living a life of poverty, chastity, and obedience to God) assigned to live in the dormitory with us. Each student had an 8-by-12 foot cubicle about the size of a small office. I shared a bunk bed with a fellow classmate, and the dormitory was set up similarly to an army barracks.

Trauma made it difficult for me to form intimate relationships with people. I began to date a girl during my sophomore year of high school while attending St. Lawrence Seminary. It was difficult to open my heart to her. Each time she connected with me at an emotional level, I broke up with her. Invariably, we would get back together only to eventually break up again. Mom was opposed to me dating a woman, especially while I was in high school and my early college years. Mom teased me about the women I dated and made me feel pathetic and dirty inside. She told me, "What will other people think about you liking a girl and being a seminarian?" I felt like crap and began to believe I did not deserve to be in a relationship with a woman. When I felt pleasure with another woman, I immediately went from my heart to my head because I told myself if I allowed pleasure into my life, then something bad was going to happen.

I believed shame and sadness drove this on-again-off-again aspect of the relationships I had. I thought, "I don't deserve to have a relationship with any girl because I am not a lovable person." I felt unloved as a child, surmising love is somehow dangerous. An unloved person cannot absorb it, just like a dry sponge cannot absorb moisture until it is immersed in water.

I made a decision after my sophomore year of high school to not become a priest, contrary to Mom's wishes for me. I dated several women over the next fourteen years. At the beginning of each relationship, I cherished the excitement of each new romance. As time would go by, I would begin to pull away from the women I was dating, believing I did not deserve their affection. I felt an overwhelming sense of shame when women became emotionally close to me. I was unwilling to make myself emotionally vulnerable to them. I believed being emotional was a sign of vulnerability and that vulnerability was weakness. I did not like feeling vulnerable in this way. The only solution for me was to break off the relationship.

Identifying feelings is an arduous process for me. I think to myself, "Should I feel love, terror, shame, pain, guilt, or pleasure based on the circumstance I am in?" Sometimes I think I need to feel something but in reality, I don't. Trauma is like walking into a freezer. Eventually, your entire body goes numb. I keep people at an emotional distance as if I were in a freezer separated from the outside world. When I do feel it is in the form of sadness, depression, and anxiety.

When I received an award or did something really well, I faked being happy. Later when things don't turn out well, I would think to myself, "I knew it would turn out this way, so why even feel happiness? I am worthless."

Imagination gives me hope, healing, and health. It stirs my creativity, keeps boredom at bay, allows me to cope with pain, and provides pleasure and emotional connections to others. I still sometimes lack mental flexibility and leave little room for my imagination to create. This arises during stressful times, and I must make a mental adjustment. For example, if my wife wants to spontaneously do something, I become anxious and emotionally dysregulated.

Generally, I function best following a daily routine. When something is going to disturb my routine, I want to know at least forty-eight hours before the change so that I can adjust my thinking. Balancing mental flexibility with discipline is a struggle for me.

I am blessed to have a wife who understands my mental health condition and the struggle I have with spontaneity. She knows when we plan ahead it allows me time to adjust and reduce my anxiety. For years I viewed this as a character flaw and felt ashamed because of it. When I am unable to change a behavior, this does not mean it is a character flaw. Instead, I radically accept this part of who I am. I have a responsibility to communicate with people a need to have time to make a decision or plan ahead to partake in an event.

I had a relationship with a boss who used his position to force me to do things I otherwise would not do. He had poor communication skills. He was very good at pitting people against one another, which allowed him to control situations and people. In order to get his needs met, he often was not transparent with me. When I met with him for supervision, he would give me instructions on what to do. At the next meeting, he gave me a different direction about the same task. When I pointed out the discrepancy he would push back saying, "I don't recall telling you that at our previous meeting."

In one such event, I went back to my department to inform staff that he changed his mind. Due to his lack of clear communication, staff believed I distorted the truth. During any interaction with him, I felt anxious, did not feel safe, and was guarded when speaking to him. Eventually, I recognized my interactions and feelings toward him were the same ones I felt toward my dad. I felt inferior to Dad, and this continued into my adulthood with other people who were in a position of authority over me. It felt like I walked around with a sign on my back that said, "I am traumatized: hit me."

From the ages of thirty to fifty-one, I engaged in several recovery programs and sought individual therapy multiple times. I experienced temporary relief but I allowed trauma to dominate my health outcomes. Finally, at age fifty-one, I found a therapist who began to help me understand why trauma had such a firm grip on me despite all my efforts to heal.

REFLECTION

What have I learned from reading this chapter?

PART THREE

BE PRESENT

CHAPTER 6

WIND SPRINTS
FOR HEALTH

Recovery Tools

My first awareness that something was not right with my mental and emotional health was in fourth grade. I was sad on most days, and my inability to concentrate and focus made learning hard for me. Have you observed a puppy managing its environment? It is amusing and frustrating to watch. The puppy is excited and scrambles for attention from each person in the room but is unable to sit still and focus. Teaching a dog to sit, lay, or follow other instructions is difficult because its brain is overstimulated. Looking back to fourth grade, my mind functioned like an over-aroused puppy, making it difficult for me to learn.

Basketball was an obsession and an escape from my home environment. I was a member of a team throughout my teens and early adulthood. As an only child, I often did not have anyone to play with so I went to our backyard to shoot hoops. Alone, I pretended I was Larry Bird who played for the Boston Celtics during the late seventies and eighties. I created a fictional game with the score tied. With only seconds remaining, I would move to a spot on the driveway, bounce the ball, square my feet to the basket, and release the ball from my hands. When I made a shot, I would celebrate the victory with my arms raised and my body wiggling. I wore out basketballs quicker than the tread on my bike tires.

I organized pick-up games with my friends; we had some real basketball battles against each other. My basketball skills continued to improve in middle school. When I became an eighth grader, I was one of the best players on the team. I received recognition in the paper and from my coaches, friends, and other people. Dad found it difficult to give me praise for my success. When I won an award, he rarely recognized my achievement. This made me sad, and I longed for his approval. I thought to myself, "If I just try harder or get more awards, he will become proud of me and I will not be depressed." I fooled myself about the depression part since achievement filled a hole inside me but was not a long-term solution to my depressed and anxious mood.

During middle school, I had a difficult time concentrating and did not have the ability to absorb information. I studied for hours to become an average student. Later, as an adult, I had a conversation with Dad about whether he recognized any mental or emotional issues making it difficult for me to learn. His response was, "I thought you were pretty normal." I said to Dad, "I became an expert at hiding the pain, sadness, and anxiety that festered inside of me."

Freshman year of high school was difficult for me; it was the first time I spent an extensive period of time away from home. I found myself sad, anxious, and depressed because I missed my family and friends. My parents were able to attend Sunday mass and take me off campus for lunch in a nearby town or they took me home, only forty minutes from campus. Mom regularly brought a care package of baked goods, candy, and hygiene products when she and Dad visited me. When I returned from a home visit, my stomach became queasy, a lump the size of a marble formed in my throat, and my depression and anxiety symptoms kicked in.

Late on a Sunday afternoon after a visit with my parents, the priest responsible for the freshmen class noticed I was struggling. He wrapped his long burly arm around me and said, "Do you need to talk?"

Immediately I began to weep and replied, "I miss being home."

He was compassionate toward me, acknowledged my sadness, normalized my feelings, and told me that other freshman classmates were experiencing the same loneliness I was.

Throughout my freshman year, sadness and anxious feelings consumed several days. I thought everyone felt this way. Coursework was difficult due to my symptoms, causing me to struggle mightily to obtain average grades. Thinking about taking tests and quizzes induced anxiety; my mind was like static on a television screen, which made it difficult to retain what I learned.

I was the best basketball player on my high school freshmen team, was viewed as a leader, and was well-liked by my teammates. Temporarily this made me feel good about myself. Basketball gave me purpose, enhanced my self-worth, and allowed me to escape the emotional pain I felt inside my body. I completed ninth grade at the seminary with satisfactory grades. I looked forward to being home for the entire summer. My excitement gave me pause as I tried to discern if God was calling me to the priesthood.

I began to realize in tenth grade that the priesthood was not a vocation I was being called to pursue. I was attracted to girls and had the desire to be a husband and father one day. I did not admit this to anyone because I knew my mom would be upset.

Prior to entering my junior year of high school, I began to date a kind and compassionate girl. We spent time at her home hanging out, swimming in the family pool, going to the movies, and stopping afterward for pizza. Mom was not happy with my decision to date since I was in the seminary to be a priest. One evening, I was getting ready to go to my girlfriend's house and she said, "What will people think about you dating a girl and going to the seminary?"

I dismissed her comment and thought to myself, "I no longer wish to become a priest."

Looking back, I understand why Mom was pushing me toward the priesthood. In our extended family, there were several ordained priests and sisters. At that point, I said nothing to my parents about my lack of a calling to be a priest. I did not want to go back to the seminary for eleventh grade.

On a beautiful sunny evening during the late summertime between the tenth and eleventh grades, my parents and I were sitting outside in lawn chairs, grilling on the barbecue and talking about random things. I used this time to speak with them about my return to the seminary for my junior year. I remember my mouth became very dry and my legs shook up and down. I was seated in a lawn chair and felt like I was going to throw up. Finally, I had the courage to say, "I don't want to go back to the seminary because I want to be home with you, be connected to my friends, and be with my girlfriend."

Mom and Dad were stunned. They pleaded with me to return to the seminary. After a long discussion, Dad said, "We are fine with you returning home for school under one condition: you agree to attend a Catholic High School."

The school was twenty minutes from our home. There was no way I would attend this school since I wanted to attend the local public school, which happened to be across the street from our home. I said, "I will return to the seminary for two weeks, see how I feel, and make a final decision."

Two weeks later my parents telephoned me at school, "So what have you decided?"

My response was, "I will stay."

Becoming a priest was not a condition for being able to remain at the seminary. I was in a class of forty students, and only a handful pursued the priesthood or the diaconate as a vocation.

In high school and college when I was home for the summertime, I ran on blacktop and gravel roads just outside the city limits of Reedsville—my hometown in Wisconsin. I followed a four-mile course surrounded by farmland and a beautiful landscape. Running helped me manage my depression, my anxiety, and the urge to binge on food. I perspired easily, which caused sweat to roll down my forehead.

When I finished a run, any sadness or anxiety I felt prior to running was magically washed away. I felt joy and happiness and noticed that my concentration drastically improved. However, the next morning when I woke, I felt the same sadness and anxiety as the day before. This cycle continued until I was fifty-one years old—and, to a lesser extent, still exists today.

During my late teens and early adult life, symptoms of depression and anxiety increased. I kept this little secret to myself. Sophomore year of high school I was one of five starting players on the varsity basketball team. This was unusual since most sophomores played on the junior varsity team. The other four starters were seniors. The seniors did not accept me as an equal to them. They became envious after the first few games because I was scoring at a frantic pace. Eventually, they became reluctant to pass me the ball.

This experience caused me to think there was something wrong with me. I did everything I could to fit in. However, as the season progressed it became more difficult to maintain a positive attitude. In my mind, I thought, "I must be bad," which reinforced the messages I told myself throughout my childhood. My tenth-grade high school classmates were on the junior varsity basketball team, which may have been better for both teams if I was on junior varsity rather than varsity. My performances made me feel good about myself. However, when I performed poorly, I became depressed. I continued using food to cope with my feelings. Food soothed me when I was depressed, anxious, and feeling empty inside. However, I binged and purged often, and I feared becoming fat. Normally I binged by eating cookies, candy bars, cake, and other sugary foods. I convinced myself that it fed the constant depression and anxiety I felt inside of my body.

In my junior year of high school, my classmates joined me on varsity. I was a first-team all-conference selection and led the conference in scoring. Despite my success, I secretly disguised how depressed and anxious I was.

I looked forward to my senior year. I was elected by classmates as student council president. This position gave me responsibilities over activities that were held throughout the school year such as homecoming, the winter carnival, and an all-school spring track event. Each class competed against other classes in sporting events. I demonstrated outward success but, on the inside, I felt alone and depressed. Basketball continued to be an important part of how I felt about myself. I noticed after a practice or a game that I mentally and emotionally felt better. It was like my brain was working again.

We had a good basketball team during my senior year of high school. We ended with the best record in school history. I received first-team all-conference, and for the second time in two years, I led the conference in scoring. Entering the state tournament, I was confident that we could win our first game and move on to the second round. The game was close the entire way. With only seconds to play, we were behind by one point and had the ball, giving us an opportunity to score and win the game. I rushed down the court and found a spot to receive a pass from the point guard. I caught the ball four feet from the basket, eyed the rim, shot the ball, and was fouled with two seconds left on the clock. I realized the game was on the line and I became wickedly anxious. A voice in my head said, "You will not make this free throw." The ball left my hands, and it looked to be on target. Suddenly, it looped around the rim several times and fell to the court. I had another shot to tie the game.

My anxiety was so high I thought I might wet my shorts. By this time, anxiety took away my ability to concentrate. I bounced the ball three times, which was my usual routine, held the ball in both hands, and positioned my middle finger over the valve, which allowed me to get a firm grip on the ball. I took a few deep breaths and shot the ball toward the rim. Sadly, it hit the right side of the rim and bounced to the floor. We lost the game. I felt terrible, tears filled my eyes, and sweat dripped down my face. My high school basketball career was over. I believe my childhood trauma had a role in this outcome. Being in this circumstance it seems logical that I would experience anxious feelings. However, in my case, it was extreme since I was unable to control my self-defeating thoughts.

I graduated in 1983, from St. Lawrence Seminary in Mount Calvary, Wisconsin. My parents organized a graduation party held in my honor. A lush bar was filled with different brands of hard liquor, wine, and beer. Several people became stupid with their consumption, doing things they otherwise did not do when sober.

My aunt and uncle had a beautiful white Buick Regal. They lived over an hour from our home. My aunt was my mom's sister. She enjoyed being the center of attention at parties. She was often dressed in expensive clothes. A rumor in the family was she would purchase a dress or other garment, wear it once, and return it to the store she bought the clothes from, expecting a full refund. No one knew if this was true, but it made for a good story. My uncle was a high school teacher and a career Navy man. Generally, he was quiet and very kind. Once he began to drink his lips loosened up a bit from the alcohol and he began to tell tasteless jokes.

My aunt and uncle were extremely intoxicated by the time they were ready to leave the party. Both of them were insistent on making the eighty-mile return trip home. Dad attempted to convince them to stay the night at my grandmother's, which was three blocks from our home. However, they would not hear of it and left before sunset.

An hour later a policeman appeared in our driveway. The officer exited his vehicle, approached Dad, and said,

"There was an accident. Everyone is fine but the car suffered a lot of damage."

Immediately Dad sprang up, got in the car, and went to the scene of the accident. When he arrived, he noticed the wreck and the trauma it induced on my aunt, uncle, and cousin. Dad retrieved all the people involved in the car accident and traveled to Grandma's so they could spend the night.

Depression, anxiety, and addiction are hereditary and our family was not immune to this disease. Some were diagnosed, and other family members had several of the symptoms but were not diagnosed. Alcohol was always the focal point of any celebration with our family and friends.

According to Mom, several relatives on her side of the family were alcoholics. In the forties and fifties, alcohol consumption was high in our family. Mom's father owned and operated a tavern in Reedsville, Wisconsin. The population of the village was approximately nine hundred people. At one point the village had more taverns than churches. Reedsville had a park, baseball diamonds, a volunteer fire department, schools, several community organizations, and a grocery store. During the summertime, the biggest event in town was heading to the softball diamond to watch various taverns and businesses compete against each other.

While I was in high school, I began to realize Mom liked to consume alcohol. Looking back at that period in her life, I realize she was using alcohol to manage her bipolar condition and avoid her childhood pain. On the outside, Mom appeared to handle her alcohol well. Due to her condition, she was instructed by her psychiatrist to refrain from alcohol usage while taking lithium. (Lithium is a naturally occurring salt that, in purified form, is used to treat certain psychiatric disorders, especially bipolar disease. The therapeutic level of lithium, the amount needed to treat bipolar disorders, is perilously close to the level that can cause toxicity, so monitoring of blood levels is required.)[1] When Mom drank, her personality became more pleasant. When she did not drink, she seemed to be emotionally distant and unable to manage her highs and lows. *Mixing alcohol with psychiatric medication adversely impacts the effect of the medication. I spoke to Mom about this but she had no intention to stop drinking. After a while, I realized she did not want my help.*

During my sophomore year in high school, I drank for two reasons: to fit in with friends and to cope with my symptoms of depression and anxiety. That is, to ease the pain. In tenth grade, I began to drink beer and Bonne's Farm wine. I drank to numb the impact of my condition. Boone's Farm wine was cheap and easy for an underage drinker to purchase. A bar outside of Reedsville had no problem selling wine to me despite my being underage. The bar owner had one condition, "You must purchase it as a carry-out."

The wine tasted similar to Listerine mouthwash. I became a binge drinker, drinking mostly on weekends until I was intoxicated. When I drank, I would get the munchies and eat until I became nauseous. Following an alcohol binge, I would wake up in the morning feeling absolutely miserable and ashamed of myself. My self-inflicted punishment for my behavior was a four-mile run to dispose of the calories I consumed.

After high school, I attended the University of Wisconsin–La Crosse (UWL). The basketball coach at UWL recruited me to play as a member of their team. Ironically, I was interested in becoming a physical education major (which UWL was noted for). However, when I found out I would be required to take anatomy and physiology I decided to pursue becoming an elementary school teacher. I had no idea what I wanted to do for the rest of my life. My motivation to attend college was to play basketball.

While in college, I continued to experience episodes of severe depression and anxiety. I did not know that frequent episodes of depression and anxiety were a sign of a mental health condition. Also, I was unaware that it can have a genetic link within families.

While walking to class one day I was overly anxious about taking an exam. My concentration and focus were affected. I also felt this way in high school before tests and quizzes. This was much worse. My stomach became upset; I felt a lump in my throat the size of a marble; and when I completed the exam, I was exhausted due to the mental energy it took to answer the questions. This anxious feeling continued throughout my academic career when I needed to take an exam or face a big moment in a basketball game. Later I realized it was not just performance anxiety.

Freshman year of college, I had an exceptional basketball season. I was voted by my teammates as the best player on the team. I was a pure shooter, which means there were a few flaws in my jump shot. I would position my feet under my body toward the basket, bring the ball above my head, raise my arms to a 90-degree angle while my eyes were fixed on the front of the rim, and I would release the ball with a flick of the wrist. It looked like I was placing my hand into a cookie jar.

During college, I had a drinking problem. I drank heavily on most Thursday, Friday, and Saturday evenings—except during the basketball season when I indulged on Saturday evenings only. When I drank, I became more depressed and noticed the negative effects of alcohol on my mental health. Another reason I drank only on Saturdays was that I needed to remain sharp throughout the week to complete my academic work. I wrote previously the difficulty I had with retaining information due to my depression, anxiety, and Post Traumatic Stress Disorder (PTSD). Adding alcohol only exacerbated my symptoms, especially my cognitive ability. Depression and anxiety were my nemeses during my entire college career. I was at war with my brain because each day was a battle to survive.

During my mid-twenties, I continued to hide my unhealthy relationship with food. Sometimes I stopped after work at Perkins restaurant to buy one of their delicious pies. I took it home, sat down, and ate the entire pie in one sitting.

In 1991, I worked full time as a coach and attended graduate school. This was a stressful period of time in my life. Near the end of the second semester in 1992, I came to terms with the fact that the relationship I had with food was not normal. I began bingeing and purging in my teens to escape the pain I had bottled up inside of me. Next to the apartment where I lived in graduate school, there was a grocery store. When the urge to binge was great, I gathered some cash and walked to the store. Once in the store, I chose foods high in sugar such as Little Debbie peanut butter bars, which were a favorite of mine. I devoured an entire box in one sitting.

I realized something needed to change because my behavior was out of control. Once again, my friend urged me to attend an outpatient eating disorders clinic. The staff were kind and caring toward me. Few men attended the program because it was primarily females who were courageous enough to seek treatment compared to men. Due to treatment, I made some progress. The behavior did decrease but it did not address the root cause of the reason I binged on food. I made no connection to childhood events or symptoms of depression and anxiety. Recovering from a food disorder is difficult because I needed to eat in order to remain healthy and alive. With other addictive behaviors—such as drugs, smoking, and alcohol—people can abstain.

While in treatment I learned how to eat, which was helpful. However, I continued to binge and purge when I emotionally struggled. I especially struggled with food when I was under stress.

Today I eat because my body needs the nutrients to sustain itself. Thankfully I no longer binge and purge on food but the urges still arise sometimes. My gastrointestinal tract has some damage due in part to my history of a food disorder. I continue to be unable to normally absorb the food I eat and get the necessary nutrients for my body to function.

Up to my late twenties, I functioned without medication, woke up depressed, and felt a heaviness inside of me. I dragged myself out of bed, followed my normal routine, and somehow pushed myself through the day. It felt like I carried around a semi-truck on my back. Others told me I looked as if I had the weight of the world on my shoulders.

I realized something was not right, wondering, "Why am I feeling sad most of the time? Why am I always anxious?"

A friend knew I struggled with depression and anxiety. He encouraged me to seek professional assistance. I attended several therapy appointments to discuss how I felt. I wore a coat of armor to protect myself from the feelings buried inside of me. At this point, I had not made a connection between my childhood trauma and its impact on my functioning. In early adulthood, I spoke about depression and anxiety like a reporter writing a news story with little emotion in the article. Eventually, I stopped seeing the therapist because I was not ready to face the darkness inside of me. I deluded myself into thinking I was fine, but truthfully, I continued to be sad and anxious and used food to cope with my stress.

Over time I learned that I could reduce the intensity of depression and anxiety by riding a stationary bike, and I continue to do so today. Riding is therapeutic for both my mental and physical health. Riding calms my brain, allowing me to focus and think. When I did not exercise on a particular day my brain had little energy to function. It's like taking an iron or desk lamp cord and plugging it into a light socket, and nothing happens. Processing circumstances and retaining information continued to be difficult. This became worse with each major depressive episode. I still have hope by sticking to my recovery plan I can regain some of the brain function I lost during my last major episode in 2018.

NOTE

1. "Lithium" as defined by *Medicine Net*, https://www.medicinenet.com/lithium/definition.htm.

REFLECTION

What have I learned from reading this chapter?

CHAPTER 7

PLAYGROUND SURVIVAL

Treatment Saves My Life

There are fond memories that I enjoyed with my parents when I was a child despite the horror behind the scenes. One of our family outings was a trip to Yogi Bear's theme park. Sometimes another family would join us to share the experience with us. I was an only child, and Mom and Dad knew I enjoyed doing things with other children my age. Friends of our family had three children, and they joined us.

When I entered the theme park, there was an enormous statue of Yogi Bear. It was the tallest thing I had ever laid my eyes on. Yogi had a green cap with a black stripe around the entire hat. He had big floppy ears, black eyes, and a doglike snout. A white collar circled his neck, and a green tie hung on his torso.

There were several playground items to climb and slide on. I enjoyed the A-framed cabin, which was the home of

Yogi Bear. Next door was a herd of deer in a large fenced-in area. Dad gave me some change to plug into a bright red machine full of corn. The machine looked like a bubble gum dispenser, similar to one you might see when exiting a store.

We had a picnic lunch that satisfied our appetites. Mom packed my favorite food, which was Twinkies. The golden cake surrounding the white cream was soft and had the texture of a moist piece of white cake.

I was very happy to be with my three friends enjoying an afternoon of fun and games. Despite my home circumstance, it is important that I recognize that my parents had moments like this when they were kind and gentle toward me. Mom smiled at me during the entire afternoon because she saw the joy I was having at the theme park.

During my second year of graduate school, I was an assistant basketball coach at Viterbo University in La Crosse, Wisconsin. The Head Coach had a similar personality to my dad. I thought if I were perfect I would receive the love and security I desperately was seeking from a man. Upon reflection, I sought a father figure to fill the void my dad was unable to satisfy. The Head Coach put me down and was condescending toward me. I wonder what his childhood experience was like. Some men that chose to coach use the profession to take back the power they lost as a child. They may have been bullied or abused as children and find revenge by verbally or physically abusing athletes.

By the final semester of graduate school, I felt hostility, anger, and resentment toward the Head Coach. I desperately needed to separate from him because it impacted my emotional health, and he triggered my trauma. I was an emotional mess and felt exhausted from bottling up my feelings. I was wound tight like a roll of carpet. I was frozen, unable to think, feel, and perform my daily responsibilities. In an effort to escape, I briefly left the team and stayed at my friend's home. While away, I received a telephone call from the Head Coach; he wanted me to return to the team. I listened to him as my stomach began to cramp, feeling as if I were going to throw up. At that moment I made up my mind that I would finish out the year as an assistant coach with him and not return for the third year. This whole experience crushed my desire to ever coach again.

When I graduated with my master's degree, I wanted the day to be a joyous occasion. I was very proud of my accomplishment, and I wanted to celebrate this milestone in my life. After the commencement ceremony, Mom and Dad took the entire family and my friends out for a meal. As usual, by the end of dinner, several of my relatives were intoxicated.

I had a hotel room reserved for the evening. Other family members also stayed at the same location. When we returned to the hotel, there was a bar with alcohol made available by my parents to those family members who joined us. The celebration continued in my parents' room well into the night. I was devastated by the behavior of some of my relatives. I excused myself to my room to take a break from the festivities. I stood in front of my window and looked out into the parking lot at a pizza joint. I said to myself, "Never again." I made a pact with myself that during future celebrations in my honor, alcohol will be sparsely served or not at all.

Sporadically for the next fourteen years, I continued in therapy. I did not have a close relationship with my parents. After I completed graduate school, I stopped having any relationship with my parents. This was not meant to punish them for their indiscretions toward me. I felt this was necessary to allow me time and space to heal and recover.

In 1991, I became vulnerable with my therapist and shared the secrets of my childhood. This led to the first of three major episodes of depression and anxiety during the course of my life. Initially, everything was dark and scary. I feared I would be unable to work in the social work profession any longer. I spoke with my supervisor about my emotional state of mind. She said, "I will refrain from giving you clients who were physically or sexually abused until you can work through some of your pain with your therapist."

God had a hand in this because I was fortunate I received support from my supervisor. Most professions are less tolerant of people with mental health conditions due to the stigma that exists in our culture.

I wanted to be in a relationship with a woman. In July 2013, I met a compassionate woman who made me realize what it means to trust another human being. I described to her my mental health condition and the impact it can have on a relationship. My admissions did not scare her away. Although, I must admit if I were her, I would have run like hell. We had a lot in common and after one and a half years of being together, we decided to marry on January 17, 2015.

As the ceremony approached, my anxiety was sky-high. I fought hard to not give in to my irrational thoughts and out-of-control feelings. Once married, I was unable to keep the volcano from erupting.

Paula is different from the woman I married in 1994 who later divorced me in 2003. My first wife was a hard worker, athletic, and I enjoyed spending time with some of her family members. Paula, my current wife, is kind, caring, and compassionate person. Immediately I became comfortable spending time with her. I vaguely told her about my mental health condition and my symptoms. I told her I became withdrawn and isolated from other people when my moods were in dark place. I regret not telling her all my symptoms or the extent of the darkness I felt when a major mental health episode occurred.

A few months prior to our marriage, I noticed my mood sliding downward. I was more anxious and irritable and felt sad on most days. I fought the darkness inside of me by appearing happy to family and friends. The whole thing felt ridiculous, saying to myself, "How could I feel sad since I am marrying my soulmate?" I should have been looking forward to this joyous occasion.

One afternoon Paula and I took a drive on a beautiful sunny afternoon. I commented to her, "I feel like I am in the desert wandering in an attempt to find myself."

Paula has three beautiful daughters from her first marriage. One was in middle school, the other was in high school, and a third just graduated from high school. I was both thrilled and scared to become a stepfather to the girls.

When I began dating Paula, she said, "We (me and the children) are a package deal." I look back at that moment and smile to myself. These four women are a blessing in my life.

Our wedding ceremony was beautiful. Family and friends witnessed our commitment to each other. The week after our wedding we both took time away to relax and enjoy our new life together. We did not go anywhere in particular but did stay one evening at a bed and breakfast. I continued noticing that my mood was slipping into darkness. I fought back against the sadness, which zapped my energy. I received short-term relief by swimming at the YMCA. As I had learned, exercise calms my brain and affords me mental clarity.

My belief was, "I will bull my way through this darkness." In a previous episode of depression, this attitude allowed me to survive the dreadful experience.

I returned to work after our marriage on February 3, 2015. When I was ready to start the workday, I was an emotional mess. I entered my office, closed the door, and dropped to my knees asking God to lift the darkness I felt inside of me. I asked Him to help me be emotionally strong because I could not get through this without Him. I was a wreck, and awful thoughts spilled out of my brain like an artist splashing paint on a canvas.

Some of the dreadful thoughts were, "You don't deserve to be happy," "You are no good," and "You are stupid." The logic was absent from my thought process. I courageously fought back, which made things worse for me.

The next day, February 4, 2015, I rose extremely depressed. I could barely make it out of bed to get ready for the day. I had never experienced this degree of darkness; it spooked the hell out of me. Fortunately for myself, I relied on God's strength to provide the fuel I required to make it through the workday. Walking into my office, closing the door as I did the previous day, I once again collapsed onto my knees near my desk. I prayed hard to God and when I finished, I was perspiring. Depression and anxiety were overwhelming me so much that I wondered if I ever was going to think straight again. With God's help, I was able to act my way through the workday without anyone noticing, or at least I told myself this.

I returned home from work to my new bride and family. After supper, I retreated to our bedroom. Paula followed because she recognized something was not right with me. I did not have any physical pain or broken bones but I knew there was something wrong with my mind. I shared my thoughts with Paula about how I felt. Suddenly, feelings burst out of me like an erupting volcano, and I wept. I remember Paula saying, "What is going on inside of you has been there for a long time."

I said, "If I don't deal with it now, I will not make it through the remainder of my life." She held me tightly, validating what I felt, and listened to me without judgment.

What was happening to me? Why did this happen now? I thought that God must be angry for something I did and was seeking justice for my behavior. In my darkest hour, I realized it was time to surrender, let go, experience what I felt, and ask for help. I was determined not to run, numb what I felt, or isolate myself from other people. I needed to turn it over to God. I made an intentional decision to do whatever it takes to find healing and peace. It was time to place a pair of knee-high galoshes on and clean up the messiness inside of me.

The third time when I was in a deep depression became the first time I contemplated suicide. I thought to myself, "The effort it requires of me to heal is too painful."

My wife and I made a journey to Mayo Clinic in Rochester, Minnesota, to see my psychiatrist. I felt the hope I had to overcome my mental health condition slowly slipping away. I was given two options as a course of treatment. I could be admitted to inpatient mental health services or I could attend a daily outpatient program. I became pretty freaked out when the doctor offered inpatient treatment. I did not want this option because I was determined to not be like my mom.

I chose an *Outpatient Treatment program that uses Dialectical Behavioral Therapy (DBT).*[1] Attending my first day of outpatient treatment, I was greeted by a team of people committed to helping me restore my health. I was severely depressed. My mind felt in slow motion—unable to produce thoughts—and my speech was slow, and I was anxious.

As I moved through the program, my suicidal thoughts slowly subsided, but emotionally I was still a mess. I had a constant bombardment of negative thoughts enter my mind. A therapist wanted me to journal these thoughts as they appeared. The therapist said, "Look at what you have written to determine if they are true and factual statements." When I did this exercise, I found they were absurd and served no purpose. In addition to the program, my psychiatrist adjusted a couple of my medications.

Group work was a major component of the program. There were several round tables and comfortable office-like chairs in the room. Usually, there were three people seated at each table. The walls were covered with beautiful pictures of motivational and affirming quotes. I sat with a woman who rarely spoke and drew pictures most of the time as we listened to a member of the treatment team teach us the lesson for the day.

The first activity was "Mindful Practice." Generally, I viewed myself as bad, unworthy, or somehow defective. I began to practice seeing myself for who I am—simply myself—neither good nor bad, but just as I am. From this perspective, all things created in the universe have a purpose, which includes me. The greatest lesson I learned about mindfulness is it can be practiced at any time, anywhere, while doing anything. The key is to pay attention to the moment, not judging it or attempting to control it. I found it freeing to emotionally disconnect from overwhelming feelings and thoughts. I eventually completed the program, and I continue to use the DBT techniques I learned in the program.

DBT became one of two approaches that saved my life, and the other was Eye Movement Desensitization and Reprocessing (EMDR).[2] During the second major episode, I took the necessary steps to address my depression and anxiety and restore my health. When I am in remission from my mental health condition, it requires me to continue to work on my recovery each day. I learned that when I stop, relapse is inevitable. I can fool myself into thinking I no longer need to remain committed to my recovery program.

Since the third major occurrence of depression, anxiety, and trauma in 2018, I stick to a daily routine to remain on top of my mental health. What does this look like? I eat healthy, exercise, write, take my medication as prescribed, spend time with God, perform chores around the house, and do something I enjoy. *I learned the best time to continue working on recovery is when I am feeling well.* Being tenacious about healing allows me to let go of surviving and turn my attention toward recovery living.

Recovery gives me cause to leap for joy. I no longer fight against the power depression and anxiety, or addiction has over me. By surrendering, I find peace. Affliction produces endurance. Endurance proves character. Proven character, hope. And hope does not disappoint because healing is poured out into my heart through the grace that has been given to me.[3]

NOTES

1. Lineham, Marsha. Washington University, Seattle Washington, "Dialectical Behavior Therapy"; https://en.wikipedia.org/wiki/Marsha_M._Linehan#Dialectical _behavior_therapy (Wikipedia February 7, 2022).
   "Through her work, Linehan realized the importance of two concepts in mental health. One of these was that to achieve meaningful and happy lives, people must learn to accept things as they are." The other is, "Change is necessary for growth and happiness." New American Bible, Romans 5:3 (Oxford University Press 1995) 237.
2. "DBT uses a multitude of techniques such as behavioral therapy, strategies that improve coping and regulation of emotion, and mindfulness skills. The significance of DBT is apparent as it is the only treatment shown to be effective in reducing suicidal behavior." (https://en.wikipedia.org/wiki/ Marsha_M._Linehan#Dialectical_behavior_therapy)
3. Romans 5:3 (modified).

REFLECTION

What have I learned from reading this chapter?

PART FOUR

RECOVER

CHAPTER 8

SLAM DUNK

Recovery Is a Lifelong Process

In late February 2015, I was in a deep dark mood. With the support of my new bride, I took action and made an appointment to see a psychiatrist to reevaluate my medications. The root cause of my pain was not fully uncovered until late spring of 2015. This major episode was my third since age thirty. After reviewing my history with me, it was clear to the psychologist I suffered from acute trauma. I said to him, "So now what?"

He responded, "I am encouraging you to undergo Eye Movement Desensitization and Reprocessing (EMDR)[1] therapy."

I was skeptical about the technique, thinking it may be a fad. I spoke to people that had experience utilizing EMDR and to other therapists who referred patients to therapists with expertise in EMDR. Their feedback was overwhelmingly positive.

I made an appointment to see a therapist with experience in treating trauma patients using EMDR. I described to the therapist how trauma forced the primitive part of my brain to become dominant. When this occurred, it was difficult to control my urges, anxiety, and depression. In order to escape, I became numb from my neck to my waist or physically exerted myself in order to release the feel-good hormones that calmed and focused my mind.

Due to negative thoughts and my dark disposition, my psychiatrist prescribed three medications to stabilize my mood. I explained to my psychiatrist how I want to cut my wrists to feel. In order to stop those thoughts from entering my mind, I said out loud to myself, "The pain is too great to handle anymore. I am tired of these episodes, and life is a bunch of crap. I just want to feel again without swimming into the deep abyss of darkness."

I attended my first EMDR session with my therapist in the spring of 2015. Before beginning treatment, the therapist said, "I will be teaching you several relaxation techniques and activities you can use to soothe yourself during the course of treatment." Some of the techniques the therapist recommended included taking a shower, listening to calming music, drawing, yoga, using mindfulness, and other soothing activities.

I began using the soothing activities the therapist taught me in preparation to begin EMDR. First, the therapist asked me to imagine an abusive event from childhood. The therapist said, "Just let the memory happen, no need to force it." The therapist handed me what looked like an electrical cord.

Each end had pads approximately four inches in length and two inches in width. The device discharged a vibration back and forth from one palm of my hand to the other hand.

The therapist said to me, "Follow my index finger swaying back and forth from eye to eye."

I obeyed the command she gave me. Soon a childhood image flashed into my mind, like a picture popping up on a computer screen. I was being hit with a belt as a punishment for something I did wrong. I was scared, I was powerless, and I felt alone. This memory made me feel nauseous. I felt a lump the size of a marble in my throat, my chest became tight, and I felt like throwing up. I did not numb out to avoid the agonizing pain, which I learned is vital to healing.

In the course of treatment, I relived other traumatic events or triggers in brief doses while the therapist directed my eye movement. This reduced the chance of becoming too overwhelmed by memories from my childhood abuse. Prior to EMDR, when the memory of a traumatic event was triggered, I noticed the front part of my brain was unable to function. After treatment, I noticed that the executive portion of my brain was able to organize my thoughts more efficiently.

As a fifty-one-year-old man, it was awful to experience these traumatic scenes after years of suppressing the emotions that went with them. There were moments when it felt like the incidents were actually happening in the present moment, causing me unbearable pain and anguish. The therapist said, "These sessions provide slow and incremental progress. This is the goal of EMDR therapy."

As I continued to heal, the emotional intensity decreased when I would recall a scene in my head. I am learning to nurture and show compassion toward my childhood abuse especially when memories pop up from time to time. In therapy, I am instructed to reach out to remind the child, "You are safe, I love you, and you are free."

My therapist said, "You do not need to reprocess each traumatic incident. However, chose those with the most emotional intensity."

Despite the despicable images, I felt safe and placed my trust in the therapist to guide me. The therapist said, "Breathe and feel the vibration of the pads on your hands." This grounded my body to safely experience the buried feelings rather than numbing out or ignoring them.

After feeling the emotions of an event, the therapist helped me return to the present moment. I noticed I was physically exhausted. Drops of sweat ran down my face. Next, the therapist asked me, "Imagine a scene when you felt safe."

I imagined Larry Bird from the Boston Celtics playing basketball against Magic Johnson of the Los Angeles Lakers on the driveway of my home. They invited me to play a game of H.O.R.S.E., which fueled pleasure for me and was a safe haven for me.

I have a high tolerance for pain. For example, as an athlete, I was conditioned to believe tolerance for pain demonstrated courage, bravery, and toughness. Those moments during my career were dreadfully painful. Those that treated me for my mental health condition utilized those character traits to help me through my suffering. With their help, I was able to gain insight into the cause of my depression, anxiety, and trauma. Initially, therapists paid little attention to the impact of my mental health condition on my body. I learned to ignore the pain inside my body and soul. I did not face my childhood trauma because I did not recognize the connection to my physical well-being.

Self-regulation is a skill that depends on a friendly relationship with my body. Without regulating how I feel, I rely on external regulations such as exercise, constant reassurance from people, medications, or holding to rigid routines. Each can be harmful to my body's ecosystem.

My wife is compassionate and nonjudgmental. She makes me feel safe when I am with her. Her support allows me to face my childhood trauma and dispense unnecessary shame and guilt.

People who suffer from their own childhood trauma sometimes trigger my trauma. When I am exposed to another person's trauma, it reminds me of my own trauma. This is a signal to discuss this with my therapist. With unrelenting efforts in my recovery, I now notice my physical sensations and identify my emotions quicker in order to prevent a deep slide into darkness. I consider this a gift and blessing.

In his book titled *Yoga and the Quest for the True Self*, Stephen Cope said, "As we begin to re-experience a visceral reconnection with the needs of our bodies, there is a brand new capacity to warmly love the self. We experience a new quality of authenticity in our caring, which redirects our attention to our health, our diets, our energy, and our time management. This enhanced care for the self arises spontaneously and naturally, not as a response to a 'should.' We are able to experience an immediate and intrinsic pleasure with self-care."[2]

Prior to the spring of 2015, I was in good physical condition except for a mild case of constipation. However, by November 2017, I began to experience severe constipation. I would not have a bowel movement for three to five days at a time. When I was able to go, it caused excruciating pain. Other symptoms included extreme bloating, gas, and an irritable mood. I began to wonder why this was happening to me. Finally, after four months I contacted my primary physician to request a referral to gastroenterology.

Over a period of several months, I went through a battery of tests. During one of the tests, the doctor was able to view the structure of my bones. She said, "Has anyone ever told you that you may have osteoporosis?"

I was referred to an endocrinologist for a bone scan. The scan concluded that I indeed suffered from severe osteoporosis. I was shocked and said to my doctor, "That is something women have, not men."

The endocrinologist said, "It is true that a higher rate of women than men are diagnosed with osteoporosis, but men can also suffer from this disease."

In the spring of 2018, I read a book by Bessel van der Kolk, MD, *The Body Keeps the Score*. He shares that when I become physically numb, it impacts my mental health. He states, "The lives of many trauma survivors come to revolve around bracing against and neutralizing unwanted sensory experiences, and most people I see in my practice have become experts in such self-numbing that they become serially obese or anorexic or addicted to exercise or work. At least half of all traumatized people try to dull their intolerable inner world with drugs and alcohol. When people are chronically angry and scared, constant muscle tension ultimately leads to spasms, back pain, migraine headaches, fibromyalgia, and other forms of chronic pain."[3]

During the summer of 2018, my weight dipped to 110 pounds. Normally I weigh between 155 to 165 pounds, and I am 6 feet 2 inches tall. When I weighed 110 pounds, people thought I looked like a person coming out of a concentration camp. I became afraid and fearful for my life. "Is it possible I have cancer?" I said to myself.

I sought treatment from a doctor who was unable to dial into the root cause of my illness. He said, "I will prescribe a medication that may help with your constipation." Finally, after trying a dozen or more different prescriptions without any success, it was time to move on.

After a long conversation with my wife, we decided it was time to seek a second opinion from another gastroenterologist. I shared with the gastroenterologist my entire medical history, which included treatment for an eating disorder at ages twenty-six and thirty. I went through another battery of tests and all the tests were negative. The doctor came into the examining room and said, "I cannot do anything further until you go home and put weight on your body."

The doctor believed my issue was an eating disorder. "How could this be the root cause?" I said to my wife.

I ate smaller meals in an effort to reduce bloating, I had no appetite and followed the doctor's orders to do three separate colon cleanses within a six-week period of time. I said to my wife, "If the doctor is ordering cleanses, how am I supposed to gain weight?" I had become literally exhausted with the direction I was being given.

Once again, I returned home defeated and dismayed by the doctor's diagnosis.

I informed my wife that it was time for a third opinion from Mayo Clinic in Rochester, Minnesota. Another battery of tests was administered and reviewed by a gastroenterologist. The doctor concluded I had a pelvic floor dysfunction. Immediately, I experienced relief because it was not cancer. This dysfunction is the inability to correctly relax, coordinate pelvic floor muscles to release, and allow a bowel movement to occur. The treatment lasted for two weeks, and I did experience a slight improvement. I changed my diet to low sugar, low carbohydrates, high protein, gluten-free, and added a half cup of beans at each meal.

After the third opinion from the gastroenterologist, I sought a second opinion from an endocrinologist at Mayo in Rochester to confirm my diagnosis of severe osteoporosis. The doctor wanted me to have an MRI test on my brain. An MRI uses a magnetic field and computer-generated radio waves to create detailed images of the organs and tissues in my body. MRI machines are large and tube-shaped.

I waited eagerly for the results of the MRI test. The doctor entered the exam room and showed me a picture of a pea-sized pituitary tumor. I became scared when he said tumor. The pituitary is located toward the front part of the brain. The tumor may invade nearby tissues like the skull or the sinuses. Due to the tumor, my body had been unable to produce testosterone and thyroid hormones on its own. These hormonal deficiencies can cause depression, osteoporosis, and gastrointestinal problems. The endocrinologist referred me directly to a neurosurgeon. The neurosurgeon removed the tumor on March 19, 2019. I feared the tumor would be malignant.

When I became conscious after surgery, I was informed by the nurse that the surgery went well. Later I was blessed to find out from my doctor that the biopsy showed a benign tumor. A large boulder was lifted off my shoulders after hearing the results. I thought to myself, "Thank you, God."

Due to extreme back pain, which began in 2018, my primary physician referred me to an orthopedic surgeon. I had a CT scan performed on August 14, 2018. The CT scan combines a series of X-ray images taken from different angles around my back and uses computer processing to create a cross-sectional image of the bones, blood vessels, and soft tissue. The results were staggering. The picture showed along my rib cage bilaterally I had at least eight fractured ribs on the right side and six on the left side consistent with multiple healed rib fractures. I also had several compression fractures along my spinal column. Lastly, the CT scan showed I had sternal fractures, which are in the upper chest area.

Previously I mentioned *trauma is not only stored in the mind but also in the body.* Physicians now believe physical conditions have a direct link to mental health conditions.

Some of the compression fractures and contusions may have occurred in childhood because the doctor thought some may be twenty years old or older.

I am teaching myself the skill of staying calm when I identify sensations in my body in order to reduce the chance of becoming numb. The therapist continues to help me cope with the mental images and feelings, mostly manufactured in childhood. I am determined to not allow these images and emotions to pose a future threat to my health and well-being.

In the summer of 2019, I began seeing a functional medicine doctor because of my ongoing dilemma with my gastrointestinal tract. I experienced minimal improvement working with a traditional physician. *My functional medicine doctor focuses on the optimal functioning of the body and my organs, usually involving systems of holistic or alternative medicine as well as traditional medicine. My functional medicine doctor focuses on prevention through nutrition, diet, and exercise.*[4] I am noticing a gradual improvement in my physical health. I am blessed to have the financial resources to afford functional medicine care since insurance does not cover the cost of this service.

Depersonalization is common during traumatic experiences. Depersonalization is a feeling of being separated from my body. I experienced the world in a dreamlike state, rarely felt pleasure, and blocked the pain. This offered protection both emotionally and physically while the blows of the belt or wooden spoon were delivered to my hind side. I continue to struggle to feel pleasure and joy. I am envious when I watch people enjoy a pleasurable moment in their lives.[5]

Prior to EMDR therapy, my therapist taught me to befriend my body. When the physical abuse finally stopped, my body continued to be on the alert for danger. Still today, my body is on high alert despite a lack of any evidence that my life is not safe. When an infant has an interruption in bonding with their mother, it can create pathways in the brain causing the child to believe they are unsafe, fearful, and on high alert looking for danger lurking around the corner. Unfortunately, this became the manner in which I stumbled through life for over fifty years.

I am finding new ways to relax and feel safe. My therapist is teaching me to tolerate my feelings and to trust I will not fall apart or lose control when feelings do arise.

I had a broker that managed my money for almost thirty years. He did an incredible job investing for me. The time came for me to combine my various investments under one person. A different investment advisor assisted my wife and me to consider the tax implications of our investments and offered to consolidate and manage all of our assists under his company. The broker I had for thirty years was a friend and mentor. As I was considering moving the funds to another investment manager, I began to think, *"He is going to be upset and hurt when I move the funds. I don't want him to be mad at me."*

Then a voice inside of me said, *"I am bad. I need to be loyal to my broker for his years of service or he will never want to speak to me again."*

This dialogue is an example of irrational beliefs that don't fit reality. My anxious feelings brought about an uneasiness to tell my long-term broker about my decision to have another broker handle our money. Eventually, I contacted my broker and informed him that my wife and I want to move the funds we had under him to another investment advisor in order to consolidate all our retirement accounts. To my surprise, he accepted our decision without incident. He thought the timing was right since he was already well past his retirement age. He did not think his brokerage firm would be open for business much longer.

I ruminated for almost a year before I made the decision to consolidate the funds. Managing our money is an area of life I continue to struggle with. Having money provides me with the illusion of security. I am sure this belief connects to some past events in my life when I experienced financial deprivation. For example, when I was growing up my parents struggled financially. My dad spoke a lot about money, wishing he had more. I wanted enough money so that I could be financially secure.

Despite the years of therapy, I continue to suffer from thoughts like these. In order to alter unwanted thinking patterns, I have messages on the walls of my office such as, "When one door closes another opens" or "Let your faith be greater than your fear." These are mental messages that help me cognitively stay on track.

Occasionally I place inspiring messages on a piece of scrap paper and place it into my pocket, pulling one out as a reminder to change a belief about a destructive thought

I am having. I listen to inspirational speakers teaching me the importance of self-love and self-compassion. However, sometimes when my mind is in these moments and the voice in my head says, "Don't trust other people," "You are bad," "You don't deserve to be happy," and "The world around you is a dangerous place," it takes mental energy to replace these old ways of thinking.

In order to conquer these thoughts when they arise, I am intentional about overriding the power they want to have over me. I am happy to say they are less dominant today than they were in 2015.

Due to my childhood trauma and hormonal imbalances in my brain, it sometimes is difficult to access the logical portion of my mind. When I feel unsafe, feel fearful, and sense danger the rational part of my brain is hijacked by the emotional part of my mind. This causes me to become rigid and irrational and distort reality within my thoughts.

EMDR has taught me to "own" my emotional brain. Becoming self-aware and tolerating the feelings of being unsafe, fearful, and in danger reduces feeling threatened by the outside world. By embracing my thoughts and feelings I am becoming free from my past prison.

For years I told no one about the physical abuse I experienced as a child and young adult. I remained loyal to my parents despite their behavior toward me during childhood. I desperately tried to not allow Mom's mental health condition to get in the way of living my life. I put on a stellar act to appear happy despite the darkness bubbling inside of me.

My identity was shattered, and I grew further and further away from my true self.

When I turned fifty-one, I was determined to be bold, not try to be perfect all the time, learn to love myself, live in the present moment, and rise from the ashes despite a traumatic childhood. I sometimes hear myself say to other people, "How did I make it this far?" I continue to intentionally choose happiness, which is not spontaneous for me since I still find myself too busy dodging the land mines of my childhood. I finally feel safe enough to voice my opinions and feelings. I am planting new seeds into my mind with the hope of finding a balance that will be forever beautiful and bright.

Let's take a step back for a moment. As a child, youth, and adult, I felt different than other people. Sometimes I wondered, "Is there something wrong with me?"

You may recall in an earlier chapter that during my fourth year of college, I decided to take action toward recovery. I sought help to learn how to manage depression and anxiety. The therapist was someone I trusted. They offered sound advice. However, thinking back to that time, I had no idea what it meant to be in recovery nor did I want to get to the root cause of my depression and anxiety.

From 2008 through 2015, I took medication but decided to discontinue therapy. In 2008, I left the Department of Human Services in La Crosse County, Wisconsin, and became Director of the Department of Human Services in Chippewa County, Wisconsin. Professionally, I functioned at an extremely high level. Personally, my inner life was a mess. I followed a regular set routine, did not socialize very much, and isolated myself. Work required a great deal of energy and emotional fortitude. When I came home from work or began my weekend, I needed time alone to recharge my battery for the next day or week. Why did I not have the energy and stamina to engage in social activities or other personal pursuits? I learned that trauma was a contributing factor. Most of my mental and emotional baggage remained in my mind and body, which depleted the strength and energy I had available for everyday activities.

I continue to be judgmental about my feelings. Sometimes, despite my efforts, things get messy in life. I am learning to radically accept this in order to continue to recover. My peers in the recovery community tell me I will be in recovery for the remainder of my life. What this reveals to me is that recovery is not a "slam dunk."

Nothing is certain to occur or be accomplished. However, I am learning that my efforts produce progress and peace. Before I have the capacity to love and help others, it is vital to love, show compassion, and be kind to myself. This is the grace and beauty of taking the road less traveled.

People with mental health conditions and addiction look normal on the outside. Anyone around you—the person walking down the street, standing in line with you at the grocery store, or filling up at the gas station—may have a condition. Any human being with a condition that you come in contact with today is fighting to find peace and to push back sadness, fear, anxiety, and so on. Because appearances are deceiving, it's up to you and me to eye people carefully and intentionally. We need to remind each other how hidden a condition can be. I try to approach each person as a delicate, breakable, invaluable member of the community. I show compassion toward people and try to be gentle and kind to them.

Jim Rohn said, "The greatest gift you can give to somebody is your own personal development. I used to say, 'If you will take care of me, I will take care of you.' Now I say, 'I will take care of me for you if you will take care of yourself for me.'"[6]

NOTES

1. F. Shapiro, *EMDR The Breakthrough Eye Movement Therapy for Overcoming Anxiety, Stress, and Trauma* (New York; Basic Books: 2004).
2. S. Cope, *Yoga and the Quest for the True Self,* First Edition Bantom Books (September 5th, 2000).
3. Van Der Kolk, MD, *The Body Keeps the Score,* Chapter 16: "Learning to Inhabit Your Body: Yoga" (Penguin Books: 2014), 267–8.
4. D. Kalish MD, Founder of Kalish Institute, (Green Dart Enterprise 2022) https://www.kalishinstitute.com/functional-medicine-for-physicians.
5. P. Schilder MD, "Depersonalization, An Introduction to a Psychanalytic Psychiatry" (New York: International Universities Press: 1952), 120.
6. Rohn, Jim. "15 of Jim Rohn's Most Motivational Quotes," www.jimrohn.com (September 2018, updated since).

REFLECTION

What have I learned from reading this chapter?

CHAPTER 9

PRACTICE

Managing, Overcoming, and Leading a Life Worth Living

One day Tom was walking in the park during his lunch hour. Twenty minutes later, he sat on a wooden bench. On the other side of the walking trail were pink, yellow, and purple tulips. Elm and oak trees covered the entire park area, some large and others smaller. He was preoccupied with his thoughts instead of observing the beauty around him. He had a furrow above his eyes.

He noticed a man strolling down the pathway. The stranger approached him and asked, "May I sit down next to you?"

Tom responded, "It's a free country, go ahead."

The stranger stood about six feet tall, wore glasses, was rather slim, and had brown hair down to his shoulders. "You look worried. Is there something you need to talk about?"

Tom was startled and thought to himself, "How does he know something is wrong?"

For some reason—let's call it divine intervention—he sensed he could trust this man. "I am a social worker that made a home visit yesterday with an eight-year-old boy. I am teaching behavioral skills to the boy's mother."

Tom became emotional and clenched his fists, and his voice began to crack similar to the sound of pouring milk into a bowl of Rice Krispies. There were commonalities between Tom and the boy. "I was verbally and physically assaulted by my parents during my childhood. When I interviewed the boy," *Tom said,* "his story triggered a memory from my childhood. The boy's symptoms were similar to mine; nightmares, sleep disturbances, panic attacks, depression, and mood swings caused by negatively talking to myself."

The stranger became curious saying, "Have you heard of the term Post Traumatic Stress Syndrome (PTSD)?"

Tom responded, "Of course; I am a social worker."

The stranger was interested to hear about episodes of physical abuse during Tom's childhood. "I was ten years old," *said Tom.* "One evening during supper I was seated at the kitchen table with Mom and Dad enjoying a meal together. Mom poured me a glass of milk to drink. As dinner progressed, I reached for a drink of milk, accidentally brushed up against the glass, and spilled it on the table and floor. Immediately, my dad slid back from his chair, stood up, and said, 'You're such a klutz.'

"Dad unleashed a serious blow to my head. Immediately there was a ring in my head as loud as a church bell. I attempted to communicate with my parents that it was an accident. Mom sat in her seat, doing nothing to protect me."

Tom suddenly looked at his watch and noticed he had five minutes to return to his job across the street from the park. The stranger said, "Could we meet back here at noon tomorrow? I would like to hear more about your life experiences."

"Sure," *Tom said.*

Tom liked baring his soul to a stranger with whom he had no emotional attachment. This made it easier for him instead of someone he knew. They said their goodbyes as they strolled in opposite directions down the park's path.

The next day was cloudy. There was a slight chill in the air. The park had very few people in it due to the chance of rain. Despite the dreariness of the day, it was spring. The earth was becoming alive with green grass, green leaves on the trees, and beautiful yellow wildflowers in the green space of the park.

At high noon, Tom and the stranger met again in the park. Tom said, "I did not ask you your name; what is it?"

"Spirit," *said the stranger.*

Spirit was getting ready to speak when a woman walked along the path right in front of them. As she approached, both men became silent because they wanted to be discrete about others hearing the sensitive nature of their conversation.

"Tom, how has your childhood abuse carried over into your adulthood?" *asked Spirit.*

"I am intimidated by people in authority, shame consumes my mind at times, and I am guarded with sharing my emotions. I fear I may harm myself or someone else when I become angry. I guard my emotions like a bear guards and protects her cub," *explained Tom.*

Tom began nervously chewing on his fingernails. Spirit noticed his behavior, "What is going on with you right now? You're eating your fingernails as if they are a snack."

Just then, an ice cream vendor pushing a cart appeared. Tom sprang up and said, "Come on; I'll buy you an ice cream cone."

Spirit immediately suspected Tom was diverting attention away from his question. Spirit went along with Tom's request and in no time was on his heels.

After Tom bought Spirit an ice cream cone, they returned to their park bench. Tom was relieved by this distraction because he felt shameful about discussing the past with Spirit. Spirit said, "What happened after you met with the boy?"

"A memory surfaced reminding me of the abuse I experienced in childhood. Since yesterday it has been difficult for me to concentrate. I have minimal motivation to do anything, and my emotions are bubbling up inside of me like lava prior to a volcano erupting."

Spirit offered, "I can connect you with someone willing to help you with your emotional anguish if you are interested?"

"Yes, I am sick and tired of being sick and tired," *Tom said as tears formed in his eyes.*

"I can email to you resources in the area, including specialties. St. Francis clinic has a woman that works well with your issues. You may want to try her first," *said Spirit.*

Once again time slipped away, and Tom needed to return to work. Together they decided to meet at their favorite park bench in a month. Tom began walking back to work. Spirit watched him for a moment and in a slightly raised voice said,

"Remember you are a good person who deserves to find peace in your life."

A month later, Spirit had an opportunity to check in with Tom. They gathered at their beloved park bench at noon to catch up on what has happened. Tom said, "I met with a psychologist you suggested. He confirmed my suspicion that I indeed suffer from PTSD. I am having intrusive memories of terrible events from my childhood. I avoid people that remind me of someone from my past, I have negative thoughts about myself, I am always on alert waiting for something bad to happen, and I find it difficult to concentrate."

Tom has a controlling personality, probably a survivor trait. To relinquish the armor he has on, he needs to learn to trust people, feel safe around them, and be emotionally stable to process his memories. Tom shared with Spirit, "When I was a kid at home, I felt edgy all the time fearing the next physical attack."

He admitted he was far from being a perfect child and did some things that deserved discipline. "Rather than another form of discipline, I became the racehorse, and Dad was the jockey. I tried to be perfect to avoid the whip being released on my backside by Dad," *Tom said.*

Tom told Spirit that the person he was seeing is a therapist. The therapist needed him to recall a memory from his childhood. "I told her, one-time Dad whipped me with his belt because I acted out in school. My therapist gave me two pads, placed one in each hand, and requested I form a loose fist. I felt a slight vibration from the pads. The purpose of the pads was to remind me to remain in touch with my body, linger in the present moment, and remain connected to my emotions."

Next, the therapist announced to Tom, "Observe my finger going back and forth, thinking only of the incident."

Tom said, "I noticed how resistant I was to let go. Suddenly, it felt like I was back in that moment of violence, and a flood of emotions rose up inside me. My chest felt heavy and a lump formed in my throat."

Tom thought he was going mad and possibly dying because the emotional pain was tenacious.

"Spirit, the dreadful part of recalling a memory is experiencing the feelings I avoided as a child. It allowed me to feel the stored emotions rather than freezing, hurting myself, or running away from the pain."

Tom remembers his dad dashing into the living room saying, "What the hell happened at school today?"

"I knew this meant a scourging with a belt. My dad whacked me across the backside several times. The harshness of each blow grew more intense as Dad lost control of his temper."

When he concluded the torture, Tom rolled over and noticed his dad's face was beet red, he was breathing heavily, and his dad said, "This hurts me more than it hurts you."

Tom remembers the pain and the sting he felt on his bottom. "My backside was on fire. Tears began rolling down my face due to the shame I felt toward myself: 'I told myself I am a bad person and I need to grow up.'"

After the first round of eye movement therapy, the therapist asked, "Are you in the memory?"

Tom said, "Yes."

He realized the mental injury this caused him. The physical bruises had healed but his body told him something else. "I noticed that my stomach was churning like a passenger on a ship experiencing seasickness," *said Tom.*

After a period of silence, the therapist asked Tom why he was smiling. "Because I have a portrait in my mind. I was doing weight-resistant exercises in order to sculpt my muscles like a bodybuilder preparing for a weight-lifting contest. Just then Dad appeared in my mind and I stated, 'never again.'"

Personal relationships posed a problem for Tom. He said, "Relationships brought up feelings I wanted no part of."

Tom was married in 1994 to a woman he knew in college. "I realize I was doing what most people do in their mid-twenties: they get married." *After 12 years of marriage, his wife filed for divorce, which ripped his heart out. Once again, he felt abandoned like in childhoo*d. "After the divorce, I remained single for seven years," said Tom.

Tom dreaded going to the second session of EMDR therapy. He would much rather have a root canal than go into childhood feelings of physical and verbal abuse. However, he recalled the promise he made to himself to do whatever it takes to find peace and wholeness. He dragged himself to the next therapy session. Once again, his therapist gave him two pads, one for each hand. "She asked me to bring to my mind another incident of abuse from my childhood. I thought for a moment, then allowed a situation to enter my mind. The therapist said, 'Watch my finger go back and forth.' The second memory caused my body to react. I began to perspire, my chest became extremely tight, and a lump formed in my throat."

He tried to emotionally create a distance between the memory and himself. Despite his effort, he had little success. Emotions grasped him so tightly that reason and logic disappeared. "My instinct was to ignore the image curtailing how I felt."

He realized extinguishing his feelings would not resolve his childhood trauma. "I stuck with it as tears began to flow from my eyes."

When the incident had occurred during his childhood, he had felt nothing. However, the memory had stuck in his head. "Bringing the image into my conscious mind allowed me to experience the feelings I cut off at that time."

His therapist said, "You are experiencing the emotions you would normally feel when the incident is happening. The goal of remembering and feeling is to reduce the emotional impact on you. Over time, your emotions about the memory will reduce enough so your brain does not go into emotional turmoil."

Tom told Spirit he continued to go over past hurts in therapy which reduced his symptoms of PTSD. The more he embraced the memories, the more he became a whole person. How did this impact other areas of his life? He became closer to his higher power, God, which brought him peace. He told Spirit, "It was like an early morning sunrise over a lake. The water was as calm as a sheet of glass."

Tom was remarried and felt blessed because his wife was understanding, compassionate, and had considerable knowledge of mental illnesses. He also began to do resistance training or "pump some iron." Apparently, six months of resistance training can help a brain from shrinking with age. When he lifts weights, he is focused on form and performing specific moves, which in turn exercises the neural circuits in his brain.

His social and family life improved. He said, "I thought about becoming a writer, so I looked for a writer's group to join. I began to write about my experiences with depression and anxiety, and share them with my writer's group. One of the members is skilled at editing. I sent him chapters to review as I finished them."

When the writing was edited and returned to Tom, the pages were full of red ink. It looked like a pool of blood that could be found on the floor of an operating room. He was open to the suggestions of the editor in order for his writing to be engaging and meaningful for those people suffering from a mental health condition or addiction.

"I was single with no children for seven years. When I remarried, I inherited three beautiful daughters," *Tom said with a smile on his face. This helped him address issues of intimacy and find more compassion toward himself and others. Sometimes he finds it amusing when his daughters bicker at each other. It reminds him of chickens picking at each other in an attempt to claim their space in a chicken coop.*

After the second memory, the process continued for six months. He said, "This was the hardest thing I have ever done. The next day I was emotionally exhausted. I felt like a kitchen washcloth, all rung out."

His story continued to evolve. He began to work on his thinking once his mind stabilized, "My thoughts imprisoned me. They bring me down and make me feel like crap. Changing how I speak to myself is a daunting task that I must work on every day. Negative thinking is ingrained in my mind, and sometimes thoughts pop up even in the best of circumstances."

Trauma resurfaces occasionally when a memory is triggered from his childhood. The smells from the memory put him on high alert. This has nothing to do with the current smell but rather an odor stored in his mind from childhood. This is a signal to schedule an appointment with his therapist to get a booster shot of EMDR to manage the intensity of the episode. This is similar to receiving a COVID booster shot to ward off the virus.

Tom and Spirit met again one year later from their first gathering. Tom looked younger, his speech was full of joy, and he had a hop to his step. Spirit said, "Tom you look like a whole new man. What happened?"

"I continue to follow my recovery plan. I treat myself compassionately, I attend a weekly Peer Support Group meeting, I have the energy to go out with friends, and I have grown spiritually. I exercise and eat well," *said Tom. Spirit thought to himself,* "His commitment and hard work, choosing to let go, and learning to trust in God has been a miracle for Tom."

Tom spoke about how much he appreciates Spirit's advice. By listening to his story and being held accountable for his commitment to recovery. He was curious to know more about

Spirit. *Then Spirit announced,* "I will be leaving the area next week for another job. I work for my dad and go to different places all over the world."

Spirit said, "I will be with you even though I am not physically present to you any longer."

Tom was royally confused by these statements. He wanted to know more but decided not to pry any further. "I wonder how I will do this without you," *Tom said.*

Spirit answered, "You have gained much wisdom. The Spirit in you will guide you, keep you safe, and continue to walk with you in all circumstances."

Spirit began to rise from the bench. They hugged one another and they ventured down separate pathways. When Tom had walked fifteen yards, he turned around for one last look at Spirit only to find he was gone.

He said softly to himself, "Who was that guy?"

REFLECTION

What have I learned from reading this chapter?

CHAPTER 10

SKILLS, ABILITIES, AND TALENTS

Strength-Based Recovery

Recovery is a process of change. People that desire to advance their health and wellness must choose to live a self-directed life and strive to reach their full potential.[1] Early in recovery, I focused on problems and failures rather than using my strengths to manage my depression and anxiety. I am learning how to utilize my strengths and help others identify their strengths in order to help ourselves overcome the obstacles of a mental health condition, addiction, and trauma.

I supported a person who I'll call "Sadi" in 2015 that suffered from depression, anxiety, and trauma. I coached Sadi to utilize her strengths to heal. Sadi had a wonderful sense of humor, a good work ethic, believed in God, and had a supportive family. Slowly she began to emotionally recover from the tragic circumstances of her childhood.

Sadi said, "The care team allows me to make decisions on the level and type of assistance I think is necessary for me to heal. The team does not impose their will on me to conform to what they think is best for me."

Sadi voluntarily met with a psychiatrist who prescribed medicine to stabilize her mood. She commented, "I began to see a therapist to address my childhood trauma. Each member of the care team consistently communicated their support to me, which made me feel safe and protected."

Sadi found employment, utilized her sense of humor while interacting with other people, and returned to church. "There were bumps in the road of my recovery; at one point I discontinued seeing a therapist and taking prescribed medications because I felt better. My team continued to support me, and, when I fell back into a dark mood, they were there to pick up the pieces." Eventually, Sadi learned the importance of meeting regularly with a therapist and psychiatrist and receiving support from her family and friends.

Healing from a mental health condition, addiction, and trauma is not an event nor something a person stops when they feel better. Those of us that remain stable for a better part of our lives must continue to practice the daily habits of recovery in order to manage our symptoms.

Identifying my strengths and using them during my recovery provided invaluable to my healing. I slowly let the genie out of the bottle. I ask myself "Why did it take me so long?" For fifty-one years, I saw my life through the eyes of a hurting little boy. Since then, I have taken small strides toward chipping away at my childhood trauma to come to terms with who I am meant to be. This allows me to not become overwhelmed by my emotions and function effectively as a husband, father, and son. I can now choose the moments when to go into the darkest recesses of my soul to uncork the pain of the past. I suppose I could have convinced myself to just take medication to survive. However, I am taking the road less traveled by engaging in therapy, writing, and support groups that aid my recovery.

About five years ago, I took a personality test called "Strengthfinders." The test revealed my top five strengths as *a connector, a learner, responsible, intellection, and a relator.* I will share with you how I incorporate (through action) each strength into my recovery.

1. *Connector:* I like having a variety of people in my life. I dedicate myself to worthy causes, which gives me a sense of purpose in my life.

   Actions: Connecting with those experiencing similar conditions that I have opened my life to learning from other people. When I retired, I decided I wanted to use my lifelong experience with depression, anxiety, and trauma to coach and support others back to health.

2. *Learner:* I like finding out about subject matter I know little or nothing about. The means of learning, rather than achieving, stimulates me.

   Actions: I seek to understand people. I have always been curious about why people do what they do. This allows me to connect with myself and support other people that ask me to help them with their recovery. I read, watch internet presentations, and attend seminars to learn what actions I can take in helping my and other people's recovery.

3. *Responsible:* I like doing things right. I do not look for a shortcut. When I commit to doing something for someone, I follow through on their request of me.

   Actions: When I have taken shortcuts with my recovery, it proves disastrous. For the last several years I have faced my suffering and pain by working with a therapist and attending support groups.

4. *Intellection:* I am a deep thinker. When I am making a decision, I need preparation time. I like to research periodicals, read books and documents, and speak to other people that have expertise in an area I want to learn about. I look for themes and consistency. I use the rule of three. When I receive the same information from three separate sources, I take it as a sign from God of the direction I need to take in my life.

   Actions: I begin a dialogue with people to process my dilemma. This allows me to talk it out and listen for feedback from other people.

5. *Relator:* I like breaking down difficult concepts into simple tasks for myself and other people. People often come to me for guidance and counsel. I fill my mind

with new ideas by observing, studying, or listening. I get facts, data, stories, examples, or information on people I meet. This helps me understand why I and other people behave the way we do.

 Actions: I am a Certified Peer Specialist (CPS). This certification allows me to partner with people on their recovery journey. I also host a Peer Recovery Support Group one time a week for those in active recovery.

If you are interested in determining your top five strengths, go to https://high5test.com/strengthsfinder-free. There may be a fee for the test.[2] Identifying your strengths to overcome problems or concerns in your life can be a starting point for you. Using your strengths allows you to become the best version of yourself.

Why am I sharing with you my strengths and their role in my recovery? It allows me to encourage you to focus your energy on what you do well rather than trying to improve on your weaknesses. For example, I am not mechanically inclined despite my efforts to become better. When a plumbing issue arises in our home, I need to have help from my father or father-in-law or hire a plumber to correct the problem. If I attempt to tackle the issue on my own, I will create a mess. When someone suffers from depression, I can listen to them. I will ask from time to time if they want to be coached to identify their strengths and how to utilize them. This helps me assist people to set realistic goals and take action to reach their destination.

My recovery care team includes God, my wife, my dad, family members, support groups, a therapist, a psychiatrist, my author connections, and my church community.

Here are examples of goals I have set for my healing:

1. Managing my symptoms by attending support groups, exercising, eating well, and taking medication.
2. Pursuing an adequate quality of life. Be emotionally available to my family.
3. Awareness of my thoughts and their impact on my ability to function. When I begin shaming myself, check the facts by evaluating their legitimacy. If not true, let them float away.
4. Finding activities that bring pleasure to me such as puzzles, writing, spending time with family, and so on.
5. Accepting myself. Embrace my strengths and remember I am a human being that is imperfect.
6. Determining the level of therapy that is necessary to maintain my health and well-being.

Once I have reached a treatment goal, I create a new one I want to pursue or continue working on the others not yet completed. Some of these goals I will work on for the remainder of my life.

. . .

Ed is a sixty-year-old man (not his real name) I met through a therapy group I attended. He invited me to be a support (sponsor) for him since he struggles with depression and anxiety. He and his wife separated. He told me, "She thinks I am too controlling. When she told me this, I was shocked."

Ed believed that this was not true. "We made decisions together when they affected both of us. When she asked me for money or she wanted to do things with her friends I thought I was supportive."

Ed attends a support group I facilitate. He asked me, "Can I give you a call to talk about what is happening between my wife and me?" *I let him know I am open to speaking with him.*

About a week later, Ed phoned me. When he began to speak, I could tell he was hurting. He spoke very slowly; he was crying and had no contact with anyone since our last support group meeting. He said to me, "I am a mess. I just don't understand why she is doing this to me. I love her very much and want things back to the way they used to be."

I listened intently to each word he spoke. I occasionally asked a clarifying question. He told me, "I am a retired business manager. I did well making the company a lot of money. I am an effective problem solver, pursue facts to determine the truth, enjoy reading, and like working outdoors. Since retirement, my mood is low, I am less motivated to do things, and I am not sure what my purpose in life is. I am uncomfortable when my wife begins to speak about her feelings. Dealing with my feelings is hard enough. On top of that, I need to offer her emotional support."

I asked him, "I wonder if your inability to support her feelings and the control of your feelings may be an issue in your relationship with your wife." *There was dead silence.*

Then he said, "I am not very good with this feeling stuff. I want to run away like a bat out of hell when she shares her feelings." *I told Ed to take some time to think about what we discussed. I left the door open for him to give me a call back in a week to discuss insights he may gain.*

Ed telephoned a week later. He said, "She exhausts me. We spoke and we went round and round about her feelings toward me and my control of her behavior."

Instead of just listening to her, he said he became defensive with her, which only made things worse. He said, "What am I supposed to do? I am more depressed this week than I was last week when you and I spoke."

Realizing he is a good problem solver, which is a strength of his, I said to him, "Let's come up with a solution that allows her to freely share her feelings with you and reduces your defensiveness when you respond to her."

Ed was very eager to repair his relationship with his wife and have her return home after moving out when this all came to a head.

"My goals are:

1. Become comfortable with handling my wife's feelings.
2. Reduce the sadness and anxiety I am carrying around inside of me."

He came up with several action steps to attain his goals. He committed to becoming a better listener. He said, "If I listen to her without becoming defensive or attempting to solve her problems, I may become more comfortable with her feelings. I can remind myself that she has a right to her feelings and not think everything she is feeling is because of me. This allows me to refrain from taking her feelings on, which increases my depression and anxiety."

Ed and his wife continue to struggle. However, Ed is a better listener, and he acknowledges his depression and anxiety are manageable. Ed is learning that little steps in recovery pay big dividends despite his wife still not returning home.

.   .   .

I am in recovery all the time. Managing symptoms is a way of life for me. As an author, I have days when my cognition is disrupted making it difficult for me to write. For most authors, this happens from time to time. Add the layer of depression and anxiety symptoms sloshing around in my head, and it becomes impossible to resurrect memories, be creative, and write. I once thought if I pushed myself harder, I could wrestle my way through my symptoms.

Have you ever received a shock from an electrical outlet? The more painful the shock, the darker life becomes for me. When I push myself to beat back my depression and anxiety, I get one hell of a jolt and become emotionally overwhelmed and mentally paralyzed. I am learning when symptoms arise that I need to slow down instead of pushing myself. When I do this I become more loving and compassionate and remind myself, "Today is an off day, tomorrow will be better." It's like taking a sick day off work.

Due to physical ailments, I notice sensations in my body. I no longer ignore them; I face them. When this happens,

I make an effort to rebalance my life. I practice self-compassion toward my body rather than ignoring the signals I am receiving. When I practice mindfulness, I name what is going on inside of me, which allows me to tame the physical and emotional intensity of pain so I can regulate myself.

In the midst of a difficult period in my life, I worked for a boss that was extremely harsh toward my work. When he did this, it triggered memories of the harshness I received from my dad when I was a child. Paying attention to my body allowed me to adjust my behavior toward my boss. For example, if he sent me an email that came across as harsh, I did not immediately respond until I felt emotionally regulated. This approach allowed me to be compassionate toward myself and treat him respectfully.

.   .   .

When I began recovery in my thirties, I did not have a positive attitude because I carried the weight of my childhood on my back. I tend to be a caretaker for others in order to avoid my own pain. This is the reason I became a social worker for thirty years. It was easier to handle the abuse, trauma, and mental health conditions of others than deal with my own pain.

Upon experiencing trauma, the cognitive portion of my brain shuts down and I fall back into my emotional or primitive brain. When I am in emotional darkness it is impossible for me to think my way out of the darkness by simply repeating positive affirmations. After long-term therapy and peer support, I have learned to use coping strategies when my emotional mind dominates my view of reality. Once stable, I can identify the emotions I feel, explore what triggered the feelings, and use positive affirmations to create a new pathway to replace the old one.

. . .

Pat is recovering from a traumatic childhood and asked her therapist this question: "What must I do to resolve the hurts from my past?"

The therapist answered, "Use the coping strategies I have taught you. When your mind becomes anxious, use your wise mind to STEP BACK, notice your thoughts and feelings, and find the balance between emotional persecution and rational dialogue. Use your strengths with the intention of healing from your past. Challenge yourself so you feel the feelings without a sense of losing control."

Pat replied, "Following this strategy will help me manage my mental health condition?"

The therapist responded, "Yes. There is one thing left for you: stop saddening yourself and let go of past hurts. When you allow this to occur, you will be able to let go of the emotional clutch your childhood memories have on you."

. . .

I use coping strategies I learned in an outpatient program I attended. I use a technique called, "Cope Ahead" of time. I plan ahead of time in order to transition smoothly from one thing to the next. I sit down and ask myself the following questions to plan for a challenging transition.

1. What activities can I rely on when I notice troublesome feelings arise? For example: excuse myself to go to the bathroom, take a walk, etc.
2. What are the warning signs (thoughts, moods, images, situations, or behaviors) that a crisis may develop?
3. What coping strategies and skills will I use; what is the thing I can do to take my mind off my difficult circumstance without contacting another person (distress tolerance, mindfulness, and emotion regulation skills)?
4. List people and social settings that provide a temporary distraction for myself.
5. List people whom I can ask for help.
6. Name one thing that is most important to me and worth living for.
7. Identify professionals or agencies I can contact.

When I write out responses to these questions, I may share them out loud with my wife or another person I trust. Then, when symptoms arise, I am able to respond without much thought. These are the seven ingredients I mix together to create a "Cope Ahead" plan.[3]

Another technique I use is mindfulness, Being in the present moment with my disturbing emotions. Initially, I found this quite difficult to do. However, over time I have become able to allow disruptive feelings to surface without the darkness overwhelming me. Each evening my wife and

I say out loud to each other three things we are grateful for from the day's activities regardless of the level of depression and anxiety I feel for that day.

At the end of a long day, I am emotionally spent. It feels as if I have completed playing in a double-overtime basketball game. For years, I thought this was normal. Doesn't everyone feel this way? However, during my early fifties, my therapist said, "This can occasionally happen to people, however when it happens on most days in your case this is not normal."

With the assistance of medication, therapy, support groups, using my strengths, and the support of my family I am able to normalize my life. For example, when I am feeling depressed, I take the dog for a walk, continue eating healthy, exercise, and put a puzzle together. I refrain from making any major decisions or doing errands out in the community because I am unable to think rationally.

Self-compassion is a form of acceptance. Self-acceptance and self-compassion seem to happen more readily after I let go of judgment and fantasizing about how things need to turn out. I intentionally remind myself that practicing self-compassion is an opportunity to move from my intellect to my heart. Self-compassion has a specific nonintellectual and effortless feel to it. If I can find myself in the midst of suffering and acknowledge the depth of my struggle, my heart begins to soften. I start caring for myself because I am suffering. I understand that I don't need to fix it but care for it.[4]

When I am asked this question, "What can I do to support your recovery"? The answer is, "listen." I am not looking for a person to solve my problem or offer a solution. You show me you care about me by paying attention to what I am saying in order to gain an understanding of my dilemma. When I experience an emotional trigger, I find it helpful to speak with someone I trust to verify whether my thinking is accurate or not. When my thoughts are inaccurate, it is because I am looking at the situation through the eyes of a trauma response.

When I process out loud what I am feeling, it helps when people respect my physical boundaries. Some examples of this include:

1. Face me at a distance of three feet.
2. Have an open posture, and refrain from crossed arms and legs. If you don't, I think you are defensive or not listening to me.
3. Lean into me without touching; this lets me know you understand what I am sharing with you.
4. Make direct eye contact with me because this is a sign I can trust you.
5. I prefer being approached by a person being still and relaxed, to show that you are able and willing to listen. Why is this important to me? I am a survivor of trauma.
6. When people get in my face, cross their arms, appear distant, avoid eye contact at some level, and seem uptight, it reminds me of how I was treated as a child. In my family, I was seen but was not allowed

to express my feelings without my parents becoming defensive, abusive, or unwilling to listen to my side of the story.

If you support a person with a mental health condition or addiction, the manner in which people in recovery want to be approached and listened to may vary from my preferences. Remember recovery is unique for each person.

Strength-based recovery utilizes my skills to create a pathway for healing. I surround myself with people that support and encourage me. I find it helpful to connect with like-minded people in the recovery community that understand my condition. My recovery team allows me to make decisions and refrain from judging me. I have peers that I trust and confide in by attending two support groups each week.

What is your next step on the journey toward recovery? I invite you to become a Super Human Being with me. BE BOLD (courageous); BE IMPERFECT (start where you are at); BE PRESENT to yourself and others; and RECOVER to find hope, healing, and health in your life.

NOTES

1. Substance Abuse and Mental Health Administration (SAMHSA), "Working Definition of Recovery" (First Print 2012). https://store.samhsa.gov/product/ SAMHSA-s-Working-Definition-of-Recovery/PEP12-RECDEF.
2. Clifton, Don, "Clifton Strengths, Strength-Based Leadership Insight Report" Gallup Inc. Copyright 2000, 2006–2012.
3. Lineham, Marsha. Washington University, Seattle, Washington, "Dialectical Behavioral Therapy Skills Training Handouts Worksheets" (Second Edition), Copyright 2015.
4. C K Germer, PhD, "The Mindful Path to Self-Compassion," Freeing Yourself from Destructive Thoughts and Emotions (2009) 101–26.

REFLECTION
What have I learned from reading this chapter?

AFTERWORD

Today, Dad and I have a healthy father-son relationship. Writing this book has been transformational for both of us. This experience deepened our understanding of the reasons for Mom and Dad's behavior when I was a child. This understanding helps me radically accept the life I have led and the person I am becoming.

Dad and I spent over ten hours together reading and processing my manuscript. Additionally, he was always open to answering any questions I might have and filling in pieces of family history I had forgotten or had no memory of. When I read the manuscript to Dad, he had no memories of some of the events I included or could not recall an event at all. In one of our discussions, he said, "I did not realize it was that bad for you."

The path I am choosing for my own recovery is unique to my personality, circumstances, and life experiences. My way is one way and not the only way. When you elect to recover, you become a "SuperHuman Being."

I hope this work will provide motivation for you to begin a program of recovery. If you are already in recovery,

I hope this gives you the courage to carry on. If you support a person in recovery, I hope this helps you better understand that recovery is unique and is a lifelong quest for each person. Most importantly, if you have already been diagnosed, this book is meant to be a road map to free you from the loneliness of your condition and to partner with me, as a peer like you, striving each day to become the best version of ourselves.

It takes a tremendous amount of courage to heal from these conditions. Believing these challenges and conditions can be overcome is the foundation of recovery. Those of us that experience healing will most likely never have a statue erected in our honor for our hard-fought accomplishments. To me, experiencing inner wholeness is a greater achievement than being recognized with a bronze bust, trophy, or medal.

I truly believe you must recover by feeling your unresolved feelings and then finding your true self: Your triumphs; your hardships; your childhood experiences; your darkness and light; and that deep inner voice that says, "You are beautiful, you deserve to be happy, you were made for a purpose."

REFLECTION

What have I learned from reading this book?

REFLECTION

REFLECTION

REFLECTION

REFLECTION

REFLECTION

ACKNOWLEDGMENTS

When I began writing my book, I had little idea of where to begin. The only experience I had writing something to this magnitude was my master's thesis, which I completed in 1991. I learned from Azul Terronez, from Authors Who Lead, that it requires a team to publish a book. I found his words to be profoundly prophetic within the first months of writing my manuscript.

I am profoundly grateful to many people who were willing to give their time and talent to help me become an author.

I want to thank my parents for the gift of life. Despite our trials and tribulations as a family, we stuck together. My dad is the one that encouraged me to write this book in order to help others realize that recovery is possible for any person, family member, and other people that support those with a mental health condition, addiction, and/or trauma.

I have been blessed with a loving, supportive, and beautiful wife. Paula has been with me every step of the way. She encouraged me during some difficult moments. One of those moments was using our finances to pay for coaching, mentoring, editing, and cover design for this book.

Special thanks to my three daughters, McKenzie, Katrina, and Lexi Stansbury, for your unwavering support during the long hours of writing. When we got together you always asked how it was going and how proud of me you are for becoming a published author.

I belong to a group of writers and authors titled, "Inklings." We gather once a month to share our writing and provide critical feedback in order to produce great books and short stories. Thanks to Peter Wagener, Daniel Cavanough, and Cynthia Tate for your support. A special thanks to James Alf who edited my initial manuscript. I will need to compensate you for all the red ink you used.

Weekly I meet with The Leaders' Circle associated with Authors Who Lead Community (AWLC). This community helps me grow as an author by offering to coach, mentor, and teach me to increase my audience through writing a book. I and my message are important, and I am worthy and capable of expressing it. AWLC helps entrepreneurs, gurus, guides, CEOs, and other writers articulate their message and take their message to the next level. Special thanks to Michelle Fairney, Sybil Hall, Suzi Hunn, Susan Kraker, Abby Medcalf, and Ted Smith. Your support and thoughtful feedback have been invaluable to me. Through this process, you have become my friends.

The Authors Who Lead Press Publish group helped me realize my goal of completing a manuscript. The Authors Who Lead™ Press Publish is a sixteen-week guided group program where I was able to get the support and resources I needed need to see my book on Amazon. The manuscript checklist helped me make sure my manuscript was ready to head into the editing, design, and marketing phases. My sincere thanks to Kim Costa, Josiah Goff, and Sybil Hall. Our weekly calls inspired me to continue moving forward even when I doubted myself.

Kim Karpowitz, Publishing Coordinator at Authors Who Lead™, was my guide throughout the publishing process. She was instrumental in assuring all the pieces of my work were completed and tasks were performed in a timely manner. Your support and coaching throughout the process were simply amazing.

The Author Power Hour community, offered by AWLC, gave me access each week to LIVE writing session(s) where I met online through the Author Power Hour community. The sixty minutes of dedicated writing time kept me accountable. I focused on a goal for the hour, whether it be for drafting my manuscript or completing the edits to finish my book. Thank you, Azul and Heather Lee Dyer, for making this time available amidst the hustle and bustle of my days.

When I began this project two years ago, I searched to find help in the publishing and author industry to point me due north. I did a Google search and found the Authors Who Lead team. You helped me see I had a book inside of me waiting to be published. You taught me to listen to my inner spirit and allow it to guide my pen and my fingers on the keyboard. With gratitude, I acknowledge Azul

Terronez, CEO and Co-Founder; Steve Vannoy, Artistic and Creative Director and Co-Founder; Amanda Toynbee, Operations; Chante Wolf, Technology; Kim Karpowitz and Emily Chambers, Publishing Coordinators; and Heather Dyer, Author Success. You were the nucleus of my team. Anyone wanting to publish their first or even their thirtieth book needs to work with this outstanding group of people. They lead with ethics, morals, and values and unselfishly serve the people under their purview.

A big thanks to Sara Martin for freely giving of her time for taking a professional author photograph for this book. Check her out at www.saramartinstudio.com.

I owe a great deal of gratitude to my therapists over the years. Especially Donna Shimoda, Licensed Clinical Social Worker (LCSW), and Jessica Johnson, LCSW both from Mayo Health System. Donna utilized Eye Movement Desensitization and Reprocessing (EMDR) to help me resolve my traumatic childhood experiences which saved my life.

When I was at my lowest, contemplating suicide, I voluntarily admitted myself to a partial hospitalization program through Mayo Health Care titled, "Transitions." I learned a therapeutic technique called, Dialectical Behavioral Therapy (DBT) Intensive Training. I became able to accept myself, my emotions, my thoughts, the world around me, and other people.

I wish I could remember everyone who has helped me heal over the decades I have been in recovery. I would like to be able to mention you by name—because you are my

SuperHuman Beings. My gratitude for the moments you shared and listened to me has been instrumental in becoming the man I am today.

APPENDIX

Recovery Peer Support
12 STEPS TO HEALTH

Hope ≈ Healing ≈ Health

1. We dedicate ourselves to a lifestyle of recovery; our lives have purpose and meaning.
2. We believe a Higher Power greater than ourselves is the path to hope, healing, and health.
3. We choose to contemplate daily how faith in our Higher Power and recovery community can bring us peace.
4. We choose to educate ourselves and find the courage to strive for the highest level of health and well-being.
5. We communicate our plan of Recovery with our Higher Power, with ourselves, and with another human being.
6. We allow our Higher Power to be the lighthouse in our lives.
7. We humbly ask our Higher Power to reveal His unconditional love and ongoing presence within us.

8. We acknowledge our behaviors have impacted our relationships. We list those affected by our behavior and whenever possible became willing to reconcile or thank them for their support during a relapse or mental health crisis.

9. We seek mutual reconciliation for a harmful action we committed and seek forgiveness from those we harmed or were impacted by our behavior. Then, let go of our shame because it no longer serves a purpose in our lives; we understand we were designed because we are loved and to be in relationships with other people.

10. We continually review our Plan of Recovery with our Higher Power, support team, and those we trust.

11. We come to recognize our shortcomings during recovery while discovering our Higher Power is the source of our strength and mercy. We learn to rely on our Higher Power for the courage to heal through prayer, reflection, and mindfulness—and when necessary, seek professional support.

12. We gain insight into our recovery through our Higher Power as we model these steps and share our journey toward hope, healing, and health with people.

Adapted From 12 Steps of Alcoholic/Depressed Anonymous by Larry Winter and Collene Spaeth. Revised: 6/5/20

YOU ARE WELCOME TO
JOIN OUR VIRTUAL

PEER RECOVERY SUPPORT GROUP

ON THURSDAY EVENINGS FROM
6:00 PM TO 7:00 PM CST.

This group allows me to give back to the people
in recovery and develop relationships with those
that attend the groups. This is fulfilling step
twelve of the twelve-step program, which states,
"We gain insight into our recovery through
our Higher Power as we model these
steps and share our journey toward hope,
healing, and health with people."

To join our free
weekly Zoom meetings,
contact Larry at

LJW@SUPERHUMANBEING.NET

ABOUT THE AUTHOR

L. J. WINTER made a commitment at thirty years old to feel better. Recovery is helping him heal from childhood physical and emotional abuse, living with a parent that suffered from bipolar disorder, his own suicidal ideation, and an eating disorder. He is uniquely qualified to guide others through their journey of healing. After a decades-long career in social work, he is now a Certified Peer Specialist who facilitates a weekly peer support group.

I WELCOME YOUR FEEDBACK ON CHAPTERS
THAT HELPED YOU MOST AND WHAT TOPICS OF
RECOVERY YOU WANT TO KNOW MORE ABOUT.

CONTACT ME AT

LJW@SUPERHUMANBEING.NET

PLEASE LEAVE A **REVIEW** ON AMAZON
SO THAT OTHERS MAY BE ENCOURAGED
TO READ MY BOOK.

VISIT ME AT

SUPERHUMANBEING.NET

WHERE YOU CAN
SIGN UP FOR EMAIL UPDATES
AND FOLLOW MY BLOG.